INTERMEDIATE WRITTEN
CHINESE
PRACTICE ESSENTIALS

READ AND WRITE MANDARIN CHINESE AS THE CHINESE DO

CORNELIUS C. KUBLER & JERLING GUO KUBLER

《进阶中文：读与写》练习册
《進階中文：讀與寫》練習冊

TUTTLE Publishing

Tokyo | Rutland, Vermont | Singapore

Published by Tuttle Publishing, an imprint of Periplus Editions (HK) Ltd.

www.tuttlepublishing.com

ISBN 978-0-8048-4021-7

Distributed by

North America, Latin America & Europe
Tuttle Publishing
364 Innovation Drive
North Clarendon, VT 05759-9436 U.S.A.
Tel: 1 (802) 773-8930
Fax: 1 (802) 773-6993
info@tuttlepublishing.com
www.tuttlepublishing.com

Japan
Tuttle Publishing
Yaekari Building, 3rd Floor
5-4-12 Osaki
Shinagawa-ku
Tokyo 141 0032
Tel: (81) 3 5437-0171
Fax: (81) 3 5437-0755
sales@tuttle.co.jp
www.tuttle.co.jp

Asia Pacific
Berkeley Books Pte. Ltd.
61 Tai Seng Avenue #02-12
Singapore 534167
Tel: (65) 6280-1330
Fax: (65) 6280-6290
inquiries@periplus.com.sg
www.periplus.com

18 17 16 15   10 9 8 7 6 5 4 3 2 1

Printed in Singapore   1509MP

A Note to the Learner

When it comes to learning Chinese, practice is essential, of course. This workbook offers you many options for practicing and polishing your written Chinese, and was designed to be used in conjunction with the textbook *Intermediate Written Chinese*, as well as its companion volumes *Intermediate Spoken Chinese* and *Intermediate Spoken Chinese Practice Essentials*. However, this workbook may be used to hone Chinese reading and writing skills no matter which textbook or course you're using.

Here are some of the special features of *Intermediate Written Chinese Practice Essentials*:

- This workbook has been designed so it can be used either **in a class** with an instructor or by **independent learners** working on their own.
- Both **simplified and traditional characters** are taught and practiced in the same volume. This means students can learn either or both kinds of characters without having to purchase another book, and instructors have the flexibility to teach a combined class where some students read and write one type of characters and other students the other type.
- This workbook provides **character practice sheets** for the 336 characters introduced in *Intermediate Written Chinese*, with complete information on stroke order and direction for both the simplified and traditional forms of the characters.
- **Reading and writing exercises** are included, such as those involving dictation and the answering of questions based on the content of each lesson.
- English-Chinese **translation** exercises are provided for each unit.
- There are **printable flashcards** for all the new characters and words, with Chinese characters on one side and Pinyin and English on the other.
- For dictation practice, a native-speaker audio **CD is included**, as well as additional printable pdf files.
- The *Intermediate Written Chinese* **Instructor's Guide** (available gratis from the publisher) contains detailed suggestions for using these materials, as well as a wealth of exercises for use by instructors in class or by tutors during practice sessions.

附注

《进阶中文：读与写》练习册专供读写课使用，提供大量的阅读与写作练习，极为实用。学习者宜与配套的《进阶中文：读与写》、《进阶中文：听与说》及《进阶中文：听与说》练习册一起使用。本练习册亦可作为任何中级中文课程之补充教材，以提高学习者的读写能力。此套教材包括一本《进阶中文：读与写》教师手册，指导教师如何使用此教材。

附注

《進階中文：讀與寫》練習冊專供讀寫課使用，提供大量的閱讀與寫作練習，極為實用。學習者宜與配套的《進階中文：讀與寫》、《進階中文：聽與說》及《進階中文：聽與說》練習冊一起使用。本練習冊亦可作為任何中級中文課程之補充教材，以提高學習者的讀寫能力。此套教材包括一本《進階中文：讀與寫》教師手冊，指導教師如何使用此教材。

Acknowledgments

I'm indebted to a number of people for their assistance in the preparation of this volume. It's not possible to mention everyone who participated, but special thanks are due the following for their contributions:

For writing the simplified and traditional characters on early drafts of the character practice sheets, Minjun Jiang, Jerling Guo Kubler, Ching-yi Sun, and Zhe Zhang.

For assistance with the character presentation sheets and related work, student research assistants Emily Chang, Angie Chien, Andy C. Chiu, Anthang Hoang, and Peter Rankin.

For assistance in proofreading the Chinese language content of this volume, my graduate student Yuqi Ji.

For assistance in drafting the paper flashcards, Nikki Fang.

For advice and assistance with computer-related work, Adam Jianjun Wang, Senior Instructional Technology specialist at Williams College; and Peter Leimbigler of Asia Communications Québec Inc. All of the Chinese language content in this volume was processed using the KEY 5.4 Chinese language software that Dr. Leimbigler and his colleagues developed.

For their careful editing and many helpful suggestions during the production of this course, my editors June Chong and Sandra Korinchak. I also wish to express my appreciation for their enthusiastic support of the project and its development to Tuttle's Publisher Eric Oey and Vice President Christina Ong, and to Nancy Goh, Angie Ang, and the entire Tuttle Sales and Marketing team for their expertise and assistance.

Last but not least, I wish to thank the students in the Chinese classes at Williams College from 1993 through 2014 for their corrections, suggestions, encouragement, and inspiration.

Cornelius C. Kubler
The Johns Hopkins University—Nanjing University
Center for Chinese & American Studies
Nanjing, China

Contents

On Disc   4. **Flash Cards** (336 double-sided cards)

Includes practice materials for these 14 topics:

Unit 11: Getting Around Taipei

Unit 12: Shopping (I)

Unit 13: Shopping (II)

Unit 14: Eating and Drinking (I)

Unit 15: Eating and Drinking (II)

Unit 16: Eating and Drinking (III)

Unit 17: On the Telephone

Unit 18: Visiting People (I)

Unit 19: Visiting People (II)

Unit 20: Leisure Time Activities (I)

Unit 21: Leisure Time Activities (II)

Unit 22: Emergencies

Unit 23: Hong Kong and Macao

Unit 24: Singapore and Malaysia

See Disc for Audio!

How to Use These Materials

Intermediate Written Chinese Practice Essentials is the workbook designed to accompany the textbook *Intermediate Written Chinese*. It offers you a wide variety of activities for learning both inside and outside of class, to help you reinforce and activate your learning of the vocabulary, grammar, characters, and related material introduced in the textbook. The pages of this workbook have been perforated to facilitate their removal for correction by an instructor (or by a tutor or native-speaking friend, in the case of independent learners). Furthermore, the pages have been three-hole punched so that, once they have been corrected and returned to the learner, they may conveniently be filed in a three-hole binder for future reference.

Character Practice Sheets

The first section of *Intermediate Written Chinese Practice Essentials* consists of character practice sheets for all the new characters from Units 11-24, for you to study, fill out, and hand in to your instructor or mentor for correction and comments. For each lesson, the first page contains the six characters in simplified form, followed by the same six characters in traditional form on the next page. Since both types of characters are frequently encountered throughout the Chinese-speaking world, we recommend that you eventually learn to recognize both, though it's sufficient if you learn to write only one type.

Being able to handwrite characters is important not only for writing but also for reading, since if you can write a character correctly from memory, you're more likely to be able to recognize it and distinguish it from other similar characters. Later on in your study of Chinese, you'll also want to learn how to input Chinese characters on the computer, but we feel it's important for beginning students to have experience in writing characters by hand.

On the practice sheets, there are two kinds of model characters for your reference. To the left, in the large boxes, are large versions of each character with small Arabic numbers indicating the *order* and *direction* of the strokes. Note that the location of each number indicates where that stroke begins. Then, to the right of the large characters, in the smaller boxes, there is a stroke-by-stroke build-up of each character which further clarifies the stroke order. The purpose of the handwritten characters is not to serve as examples of beautiful calligraphy, but rather to instruct learners in accurate and legible writing of the characters, as written with pencil or pen by ordinary Chinese writers today.

Be sure to follow the correct stroke order and direction. If you don't, your characters will not only look wrong, but you might have difficulty using dictionaries, since these are traditionally based on the number of strokes in characters and character components. The accuracy of handwriting recognition software might also be affected if strokes are written in the wrong order and direction. Furthermore, if you're not familiar with correct stroke order, you may in the future have problems reading and writing Chinese cursive script, since the way strokes are connected is closely related to the order and direction of the individual strokes.

Beginning with the first box after the end of the stroke-by-stroke build-up, you should write the *entire character* in each empty box until all the boxes for that character have been filled. Write slowly and carefully, often referring back to the stroke direction and stroke order of the models. We recommend that you use either a number 2 pencil, or a black or blue pen. As you write each character, say its pronunciation out loud and think of the meaning. You'll probably want to have your textbook open for reference. Many learners find it helpful to write on the practice sheets the Pinyin and basic English meaning of each character to the left of the large character.

Even though there is an agreed-upon stroke order for the majority of characters, there exists a small number of characters that have common alternate stroke orders, for example, the character 方. For the sake of consistency, in the case of simplified characters we follow the stroke order promulgated by the Working Committee on National Language and Script, published in Beijing by Yuwen Chubanshe as 现代汉语通用字笔顺规范 (5th printing 1999). In the case of traditional characters, we follow the stroke order promulgated by the Committee on the Promotion of Mandarin, published in Taipei by the Ministry of Education as 常用國字標準字筆順手冊 (3rd revised printing 2008).

Reading and Writing Exercises

This book includes reading and writing exercises for each of the four parts of every unit of *Intermediate Written Chinese*. The first section consists of three phrases or sentences for dictation*. You should listen to the CD and transcribe what you hear using Chinese characters. Since this is for practice and not a test, you're encouraged to listen as many times as you wish and, when needed, to consult your textbook or the glossaries at the end of the book.

The second section includes four questions that you should answer using Chinese characters. Some of the questions are based on portions of the corresponding lesson in *Intermediate Written Chinese*, which you should refer to as you answer the questions, while other questions are addressed to you, the learner, and may be answered any way you wish.

Translation Exercises

Ten phrases or sentences for translation from English to Chinese have been included for each unit of *Intermediate Written Chinese*. The purpose of the translation exercises is to provide you with additional practice in writing the characters, using the grammar patterns, and practicing the important vocabulary of the unit, and to serve as a check of mastery over the material. Completing the translation exercises will be helpful to you in reviewing for the unit tests.

The sentences should be translated into Chinese characters with correct punctuation in the blank space that has been left under each sentence. The English in the translation exercises is in some places purposely somewhat stilted, to guide you toward the correct Chinese translation. If you've forgotten the Chinese equivalent for an English word or grammar pattern, you can consult the various glossaries and indices in the back of *Intermediate Written Chinese*.

It's recommended that the instructor correct and return the translation exercises to students before the test on the corresponding unit, so that any remaining problems can be identified and addressed in a timely manner. Students should carefully study the instructor's corrections, making sure they understand the reason for any errors, and then file the corrected exercises for later reference.

---

* Scripts for the dictation exercises are included in the *Instructor's Guide for Intermediate Written Chinese*.

Flash Cards

Flash cards are an excellent aid in memorization. They work based on the principle of spaced repetition, that is, gradually increasing the interval between each time that you recall information correctly. We recommend that you take along several dozen flash cards from *Intermediate Written Chinese Practice Essentials* wherever you go. Use the extra time you have while waiting in line, on a bus, or before classes to study the flash cards. You can look at the character side and test yourself on the pronunciation and meaning of the characters, or you can look at the English on the other side and test yourself on the correct spoken form and characters. Your goal should be to identify those characters and words you still have problems with and remove them from the larger set for special study.

The flash cards have been designed with Chinese characters (simplified and traditional) on one side, and Pinyin and English on the other side. Both the new characters of each lesson and the individual words written with those characters are included on the flash cards. The lower left-hand corner on both sides of every card has the unit and section number, while the lower right-hand corner has the character number. Due to page limitations and in an effort to control costs, the paper flash cards have been included on the CD for users to print out for themselves as needed. The flash cards should be carefully printed—first all the pages with Chinese characters, then, on the other side, the pages with Pinyin and English, after which each page of eight flash cards can be cut apart with a paper cutter or scissors.

Unit 11, Part 3: Character Practice Sheet (Simplified Characters)

NAME _____ COURSE _____ DATE _____

转	一	七	车	车	车	车	转	转		
跟	丨	口	口	口	무	足	足	足	足	足
	趴	跟	跟							
讲	丶	讠	讠	讠	讲	讲				
具	丨	口	月	月	目	且	具	具		
手	丿	二	三	手						
房	丶	冖	冖	户	户	户	房	房		

Unit 11, Part 3: Character Practice Sheet (Traditional Characters)

NAME _____ COURSE _____ DATE _____

轉	一	一	亓	戸	白	亘	車	車	軒	軒
	車	車	轉	轉	轉	轉	轉	轉		
跟	'	口	口	足	足	足	跟	跟	跟	跟
	跟	跟	跟							
講	'	二	亠	言	言	言	言	言	言	言
	言	講	講	講	講	講	講			
具	丨	冂	月	月	目	且	具	具		
手	'	二	三	手						
房	'	厂	戸	戸	戸	戶	房	房		

Unit 11, Part 4: Character Practice Sheet (Simplified Characters)

NAME _____　COURSE _____　DATE _____

加	フ	力	加	加	加			
油	、	゛	シ	氵	汀	沖	油	油
满	、	゛	氵	沪	浐	进	洴	満 洪
	满	满	满					
特	ノ	⌐	牛	牛	牛	牜	牜	特 特 特
价	ノ	亻	亻	价	价	价		
停	ノ	亻	亻	广	仁	仃	仃	停 停 停
	停							

Unit 11, Part 4: Character Practice Sheet (Traditional Characters)

NAME _____ COURSE _____ DATE _____

加								
加	コ	カ	加	加	加			
油	丶	冫	氵	氵	汁	泊	油	油
滿	丶	冫	氵	汀	汁	汁	洪	洪	満
	満	滿	滿	滿				
特	丿	宀	牛	牛	牛	牛	牛	特	特
價	丿	亻	亻	亻	侜	價	價	價	價
	價	價	價	價	價			
停	丿	亻	亻	亻	庁	佇	佇	停	停
	停							

Unit 12, Part 1: Character Practice Sheet (Simplified Characters)

NAME _____ COURSE _____ DATE _____

根	一	十	才	木	杧	杧	杷	根	根	根
拿	丿	人	스	슷	슷	合	合	仚	仝	拿
专	一	二	专	专						
业	丨	丨丨	刂丨	业	业					
办	フ	力	办	办						
法	丶	丶	氵	氵	汁	汢	法	法		

Unit 12, Part 1: Character Practice Sheet (Traditional Characters)

NAME _____ COURSE _____ DATE _____

根	一	十	才	才	村	柙	柙	根	根	根
拿	丿	人	仐	今	合	合	冷	侖	盒	拿
專	一	一	一	百	百	甫	車	車	重	專
	專									
業	丶	丷	业	业	业	业	业	苹	茔	辇
	苹	業	業							
辦	丶	亠	立	立	立	辛	亲	勃	勃	勃
	勃广	勃广	新宀	新立	新並	新辛				
法	丶	冫	氵	汀	汁	汢	法	法		

Unit 12, Part 2: Character Practice Sheet (Simplified Characters)

NAME _____   COURSE _____   DATE _____

想	一	十	才	木	利	机	相	相	相
	想	想	想						
种	丿	二	千	千	禾	利	和	种	
书	一	乛	书	书					
些	丨	卜	止	止	此	此	些		
报	一	十	才	打	护	扔	报		
纸	乙	纟	纟	纟	纟	纸	纸		

Unit 12, Part 2: Character Practice Sheet (Traditional Characters)

NAME _____ COURSE _____ DATE _____

想	一	十	才	木	机	机	相	相	相
	想	想	想						
種	ノ	ニ	千	禾	禾	利	利	秆	秳
	種	種	種	種					
書	フ	フ	ヨ	ヨ	聿	書	書	書	書
些	｜	ト	ｌト	止	此	此	此	些	
報	一	十	土	去	去	去	幸	幸	報
	報	報							
紙	｀	幺	幺	幺	糸	糸	紅	紅	紙

Unit 12, Part 3: Character Practice Sheet (Simplified Characters)

NAME _____ COURSE _____ DATE _____

才	一	十	才						
斤	ノ	ー	ケ	斤					
菜	一	十	艹	艹	艹	艹	苧	苹	菜
	菜								
白	ノ	イ	冂	白	白				
保	ノ	イ	仁	仃	仴	仴	伴	保	
证	丶	讠	订	订	证	证	证		

Unit 12, Part 3: Character Practice Sheet (Traditional Characters)

NAME _____ COURSE _____ DATE _____

才	一	十	才						
斤	`	´	斤	斤					
菜	`	十	艹	艹	艹	艹	芯	菥	苹
	苹	菜							
白	`	´	白	白	白				
保	`	´	个	们	伄	但	伴	保	保
證	`	亠	亠	言	言	言	訂	訂	訂
	訂	訊	訨	誈	諮	諮	證	證	證

Unit 12, Part 4: Character Practice Sheet (Simplified Characters)

NAME _____   COURSE _____ DATE _____

总	丶	丷	丷	丷	台	台	总	总	总	
包	丿	勹	勺	勺	包					
水	亅	刁	刁	水						
果	丨	冂	冂	日	旦	甲	果	果		
语	丶	讠	讠	讠	语	语	语	语		
言	丶	亠	亖	言	言	言	言			

Unit 12, Part 4: Character Practice Sheet (Traditional Characters)

NAME _____ COURSE _____ DATE _____

總	ㄑ	ㄠ	ㄠ	ㄠ	ㄠ	ㄠ	ㄠ	糸	納	納
	納	納	總	總	總	總	總			
包	ノ	ㄅ	勹	勽	包					
水	㇚	刂	才	水						
果	丨	冂	日	日	旦	甲	果	果		
語	丶	二	言	言	言	言	訂	訂	訝
	語	語	語	語						
言	丶	二	言	言	言	言				

Unit 13, Part 1: Character Practice Sheet (Simplified Characters)

NAME _____ COURSE _____ DATE _____

切	一	七	切	切					
肉	丨	冂	内	内	肉	肉			
牛	丿	一	二	牛					
极	一	十	才	木	杧	极	极		
食	丿	人	仐	今	今	仺	食	食	食
品	丨	冂	口	尸	品	品	品	品	品

Unit 13, Part 1: Character Practice Sheet (Traditional Characters)

NAME _____ COURSE _____ DATE _____

切	一	七	切	切				
肉	一	冂	内	内	肉	肉		
牛	丿	𠂉	𠂇	牛				
極	一	十	才	木	朽	朽	朽	朽	柯	柯
	極	極	極					
食	丿	人	今	今	今	會	食	食
品	丶	口	口	尸	品	品	品	品	品

Unit 13, Part 2: Character Practice Sheet (Simplified Characters)

NAME _____   COURSE _____   DATE _____

土	一	十	土					
节	一	十	艹	节	节			
入	丿	入						
主	丶	亠	亖	手	主			
意	丶	亠	士	产	立	产	音	音	音
	意	意	意					
思	丨	冂	冂	田	田	思	思	思

Unit 13, Part 2: Character Practice Sheet (Traditional Characters)

NAME _____   COURSE _____   DATE _____

土	一	十	土					

節	ノ	⺈	⺮	⺮	竹	竹	笁	笁	節
	節	節	節						

入	ノ	入						

主	丶	亠	二	干	主			

意	丶	亠	立	立	立	产	音	音	音
	意	意	意						

思	丨	冂	曰	毌	田	田	思	思	思

Unit 13, Part 3: Character Practice Sheet (Simplified Characters)

NAME _____   COURSE _____   DATE _____

双	乛 又 双 双
鞋	一 十 艹 艹 艹 艹 苩 苩 革 革 革 革 鞋 鞋 鞋
黑	丨 冂 冂 冃 四 甲 里 黑 黑 黑 黑
色	丿 𠂊 刍 刍 色 色
穿	丶 八 宀 宀 穴 空 空 穿 穿
算	丿 𠂉 𣥂 𥫗 𥫗 𥫗 竹 竺 笡 笡 笪 筧 算 算

Unit 13, Part 3: Character Practice Sheet (Traditional Characters)

NAME _____ COURSE _____ DATE _____

雙	ノ	イ	亻	亻	亻	乍	伖	隹	隹	隹
	雙	雙	雙	雙	雙	雙	雙	雙		
鞋	一	十	廿	廿	艹	苦	莒	莒	革	革
	革	鞋	鞋	鞋	鞋					
黑	丨	冂	冂	日	日	旦	甲	里	里	黑
	黑	黑								
色	ノ	ク	ク	名	多	色				
穿	丶	八	宀	宀	穴	空	空	穿	穿	
算	ノ	⺈	尺	灯	竹	竹	竹	笁	笪	筲
	筲	笪	算	算						

Unit 13, Part 4: Character Practice Sheet (Simplified Characters)

NAME _____   COURSE _____   DATE _____

应	、	宀	广	庀	应	应	应			
该	、	讠	讠	讠	该	该	该	该		
衣	、	宀	礻	衣	衣	衣				
服	丿	刀	月	月	服	服	服	服		
如	〈	乂	女	如	如	如				
内	丨	冂	内	内						

Unit 13, Part 4: Character Practice Sheet (Traditional Characters)

NAME _____   COURSE _____   DATE _____

| 應 | 、 | 一 | 广 | 广 | 疒 | 庐 | 府 | 府 | 府 | 庹 |
| 庹 | 麻 | 雁 | 雁 | 應 | 應 | 應 | | | |

| 該 | 、 | 二 | 亠 | 言 | 言 | 言 | 言 | 言 | 訁 | 訁 |
| 訪 | 該 | 該 | | | | | | | |

| 衣 | 、 | 一 | 广 | 衣 | 衣 | 衣 | | | | |
| | | | | | | | | | |

| 服 | 丿 | 刀 | 月 | 月 | 月 | 肌 | 服 | 服 | | |
| | | | | | | | | | |

| 如 | く | 女 | 女 | 女 | 如 | 如 | | | | |
| | | | | | | | | | |

| 內 | 丨 | 冂 | 內 | 內 | | | | | | |
| | | | | | | | | | |

Unit 14, Part 1: Character Practice Sheet (Simplified Characters)

NAME _____ COURSE _____ DATE _____

随	了 随	阝	阝	阝	阝	防	陌	陌	随
便	丿	亻	亻	扩	佰	佰	佰	便	便
用	丿	刀	月	月	用				
够	丿 够	勹	勹	句	句	句	够	够	够
爸	丶	八	八	父	尒	爷	爷	爸	
妈	乚	乆	女	奵	妈	妈			

Unit 14, Part 1: Character Practice Sheet (Traditional Characters)

NAME _____   COURSE _____   DATE _____

隨	ㄱ	了	阝	阝一	阝广	阝产	阝左	阝左	陉	隋
	阝隋	隋	隨	隨	隨	隨				
便	丿	亻	仁	仁	行	佰	佰	便	便	
用	丿	冂	月	月	用					
夠	丿	ク	夕	夕	多	多	多'	夠	夠	夠
	夠									
爸	丿	八	父	父	爷	爷	爸	爸		
媽	く	女	女	奵	奵	妒	妒	娲	媽	媽
	媽	媽	媽							

Unit 14, Part 2: Character Practice Sheet (Simplified Characters)

NAME _____ COURSE _____ DATE _____

受	一	´	⼂	⼃	⼂⼃	爫	受	受	
米	﹀	﹀﹀	⼆	⺶	�米	米			
系	⼀	乛	幺	幺	系	系	系		
急	ノ	⼓	刍	刍	刍	刍	急	急	急
喝	⼁	⼕	⼝	叮	叩	呵	呵	喝	喝
	喝	喝							
酒	﹀	﹀	氵	汀	汀	洒	洒	酒	酒

Unit 14, Part 2: Character Practice Sheet (Traditional Characters)

NAME _____   COURSE _____   DATE _____

受	´	`	⺈	⺤	⺥	灬	严	受	
米	`	⺀	⺍	半	米	米			
係	ノ	亻	亻	伫	侉	侉	侉	係	係
急	´	⺈	刍	刍	刍	刍	急	急	急
喝	l	�口	口	叮	吖	吗	唱	唱	喝	喝
	喝	喝							
酒	`	⺀	⺡	汀	沂	洒	洒	洒	酒

Unit 14, Part 3: Character Practice Sheet (Simplified Characters)

NAME _____   COURSE _____   DATE _____

桌	丶	宀	广	占	占	卓	卓	卓	桌
席	丶	宀	广	广	庐	庐	庐	庐	席
参	𠃋	厶	厶	幺	矢	矢	参	参	
每	丿	宀	𠂉	每	每	每	每		
元	一	二	亓	元					
做	丿	亻	亻	什	仂	估	估	估	做
	做								

Unit 14, Part 3: Character Practice Sheet (Traditional Characters)

NAME _____ COURSE _____ DATE _____

桌	丶	卜	上	占	占	卣	卓	卓	桌
席	丶	广	广	广	庐	庐	庐	席	席
參	ㄥ	ㄥ	厶	厽	厽	厽	叅	叅	叅	參
參								
每	ノ	乍	乍	每	每	每	每		
元	一	二	元	元					
做	ノ	亻	什	什	估	估	做	做	做
做								

Unit 14, Part 4: Character Practice Sheet (Simplified Characters)

NAME _____   COURSE _____   DATE _____

自	´	⼁	⼔	自	自	自				
己	㇆	㇇	己							
风	ノ	几	凡	风						
味	⼁	⼕	口	口	吋	叻	呋	味		
由	⼁	门	门	由	由					
留	´	⼛	丝	幻	幼	留	留	留	留	留

Unit 14, Part 4: Character Practice Sheet (Traditional Characters)

NAME _____   COURSE _____   DATE _____

自	ノ	イ	自	自	自	自			
己	ㄱ	コ	己						
風	ノ	几	凡	凧	凬	同	風	風	風
味	ヽ	口	口	口一	口二	吽	味		
由	ノ	冂	月	由	由				
留	ノ	て	亾	幼	切	叼	叼	留	留

Unit 15, Part 1: Character Practice Sheet (Simplified Characters)

NAME _____   COURSE _____   DATE _____

非	丨	丿	刲	刲	刲	非	非	非	

常	丶	丷	丷	丷	丷	丷	常	常	常
	常								

简	丿	𠂉	𠂉	𠂉	竹	竹	竹	竹	简
	简	简	简						

单	丶	丷	丷	丷	单	单	单	单	

句	丿	勹	勹	句	句				

活	丶	丷	氵	氵	浐	汗	活	活	

Unit 15, Part 1: Character Practice Sheet (Traditional Characters)

NAME _____　COURSE _____　DATE _____

非	ノ	ヲ	ヲ	ヺ	ヺ	非	非	非	
常	ヽ	ソ	ソ	ゾ	严	浐	常	常	常
	常								
簡	ノ	ト	ド	犲	竹	竺	笁	竻	筍 筍
	筍	筍	筍	筍	簡	簡	簡	簡	
單	丶	口	口	叮	叩	吅	甼	罒	罒 罒
	罌	單							
句	ノ	ク	勹	句	句				
活	丶	丶	氵	氵	汘	汗	沽	活	

Unit 15, Part 2: Character Practice Sheet (Simplified Characters)

NAME _____   COURSE _____   DATE _____

各	ノ	ク	夂	冬	各	各				
客	＼	宀	宀	宁	岁	宊	客	客		
习	コ	刁	习							
惯	＼	＼	忄	忙	忄	忄	忄	忄	惯	惯
	惯									
认	＼	讠	认	认						
识	＼	讠	讠	识	识	识	识			

Unit 15, Part 2: Character Practice Sheet (Traditional Characters)

NAME _____ COURSE _____ DATE _____

各	㇐	㇇	夂	冬	各	各			
客	㇔	㇔	宀	宀	宕	安	宊	客	客
習	㇆	㇗	习	习	羽	羽	羽	羽	習	習
	習								
慣	㇔	㇑	忄	忄	忄	忄	忄	忄	慣	慣
	慣	慣	慣	慣					
認	㇔	㇐	亠	言	言	言	訂	訂	認
	認	認	認	認					
識	㇔	㇐	亠	言	言	言	言	訂	訂
	訂	評	評	諳	諳	識	識	識	

Unit 15, Part 3: Character Practice Sheet (Simplified Characters)

NAME _____   COURSE _____   DATE _____

把	一	十	扌	扫	扣	扣	把		
夫	一	二	丰	夫					
感	一	厂	厂	厈	咸	咸	咸	咸	咸
	感	感	感						
及	丿	乃	及						
更	一	丆	百	百	百	更	更		
笑	丿	𠂉	𠂉	𠂆	𥫗	𥫗	笃	竿	笑

Unit 15, Part 3: Character Practice Sheet (Traditional Characters)

NAME _____ COURSE _____ DATE _____

把	一	寸	扌	扣	扣	扣	把		
夫	一	二	夫	夫					
感	一	厂	厂	尽	后	后	咸	咸	咸
	感	感	感						
及	丿	乃	及	及					
更	一	一	百	百	百	更	更		
笑	丿	卜	片	竹	竹	竹	笉	竿	笑

Unit 15, Part 4: Character Practice Sheet (Simplified Characters)

NAME _____ COURSE _____ DATE _____

愿	一	厂	厂	厂	厏	戶	盾	原	原	原
	原	愿	愿	愿					
当	丨	丷	丷	业	当	当			
除	了	阝	阝	阼	阼	除	除	除	除
让	丶	讠	让	让	让				
调	丶	讠	讠	调	调	调	调	调	调
料	丶	丷	丷	半	米	米	米	料	料

Unit 15, Part 4: Character Practice Sheet (Traditional Characters)

NAME _____ COURSE _____ DATE _____

願	一	厂	厂	厈	厗	沶	盾	原	原
	原	原	原	原	願	願	願	願	願
當	丶	丷	丷	少	씨	씨	常	営	営	営
	営	常	當						
除	乛	了	阝	阝	阝人	阶	除	除	除
讓	丶	亠	二	言	言	言	言	言	言	言
	言	言	誹	誹	譜	譜	譚	譁	譲	讓
	讓	讓	讓	讓					
調	丶	亠	二	言	言	言	訁	訊	訊
	訊	訊	調	調	調				
料	丶	丷	丷	半	米	米	米	米	料	料

Unit 16, Part 1: Character Practice Sheet (Simplified Characters)

NAME _____ COURSE _____ DATE _____

而	一	一	厂	厂	而	而	而		
且	丨	冂	月	月	且				
鱼	丿	卢	仫	仒	鱼	角	鱼	鱼	
改	乛	乛	己	己	孜	改	改		
务	丿	夂	夂	务	务				
员	丶	冂	口	尸	吕	员	员		

Unit 16, Part 1: Character Practice Sheet (Traditional Characters)

NAME _____   COURSE _____   DATE _____

而	一	一	广	丙	而	而			
且	丨	冂	月	月	且				
魚	丿	ク	ケ	夕	名	角	甴	魚	魚	魚
	魚								
改	フ	ㄱ	己	己	攺	改	改		
務	フ	マ	マ	予	矛	矛	矛	矜	教	務
	務								
員	丶	丶	口	口	尸	吕	吕	月	員	員	員

Unit 16, Part 2: Character Practice Sheet (Simplified Characters)

NAME _____ COURSE _____ DATE _____

替	一	二	夫	夫	夫丶	夫二	扶	扶	扶	替
	替	替							
接	一	十	扌	扩	扩	扩	护	护	挼	接
	接								
敢	フ	ユ	予	予	予	耳	耳	取	敢	敢
	敢								
量	丨	冂	曰	日	旦	早	昌	昌	昌	畾
	量	量							
深	丶	丶	氵	氵	氵	泬	泬	泙	深	深
	深								
石	一	丆	丆	石	石					

Unit 16, Part 2: Character Practice Sheet (Traditional Characters)

NAME _____ COURSE _____ DATE _____

替	一	二	丰	夫	扶	夫二	扶	扶	替
	替	替							
接	一	亍	扌	扩	扩	护	护	挼	接
	接								
敢	一	丁	工	于	开	丏	百	耳	耴
	耴	敢							
量	丶	口	口	日	旦	昊	昌	昌	量
	量	量							
深	丶	冫	氵	氵	沪	沪	深	深	深
	深								
石	一	丁	了	石	石				

Unit 16, Part 3: Character Practice Sheet (Simplified Characters)

NAME _____   COURSE _____   DATE _____

预	マ	マ	孑	予	予	预	预	预	预
爱	一	爫	爫	爫	爫	爫	严	受	爱
步	丨	卜	止	止	屮	步	步		
数	丶	丷	丷	半	米	米	米	米	数
数	数	数							
紧	丨	刂	刂	収	坚	坚	紧	紧	紧
啊	丨	冂	口	叼	叼	啊	啊	啊	啊

Unit 16, Part 3: Character Practice Sheet (Traditional Characters)

NAME _____ COURSE _____ DATE _____

預	フ	マ	ヌ	予	予	予	預	預	預	預
	預	預	預							
愛	ノ	ヘ	⺌	⺍	⺍	爫	爫	悉	悉	悉
	愛	愛	愛							
步	⼁	⺊	⺊	止	牛	步	步			
數	⼂	⼞	⼞	⽥	串	昌	昌	婁	婁	婁
	婁	婁	數	數	數					
緊	一	⼅	丂	丏	丐	臣	臣	臤	臤	堅
	堅	緊	緊	緊						
啊	⼂	口	口	叮	叮	叼	叼	叼	叼	啊
	啊									

Unit 16, Part 4: Character Practice Sheet (Simplified Characters)

NAME _____ COURSE _____ DATE _____

代	丿	亻	仁	代	代				
课	丶	讠	订	诃	谍	误	评	课	课
馆	丿	𠂊	饣	饣	饣	馆	馆	馆	馆
虽	丨	冂	口	尸	吕	吊	虽	虽	
茶	一	十	艹	艼	芡	苯	苿	茶	茶
乐	一	丆	乐	乐	乐				

Unit 16, Part 4: Character Practice Sheet (Traditional Characters)

NAME _____   COURSE _____   DATE _____

代	ノ	イ	仁	代	代				

課	丶	亠	亠	言	言	言	言	訂	訶	訶
	訶	誤	評	課	課					

館	ノ	人	亼	今	今	合	食	食	食	食
	飣	館	館	館	館	館				

雖	丶	口	口	呈	吕	吕	吊	虽	虽	虽
	虬	虬	虬	虾	虽	雖	雖			

茶	丶	十	十	艹	艹	茫	苶	苶	茅	茶

樂	ノ	イ	白	白	白	伯	帛	細	細	細
	樂	樂	樂	樂	樂					

Unit 17, Part 1: Character Practice Sheet (Simplified Characters)

NAME _____ COURSE _____ DATE _____

坏	一	十	土	圵	圱	坏	坏		
提	一	十	扌	扩	护	护	担	捍	捍
	提	提							
际	了	阝	阝	阝	阽	阶	际		
音	丶	亠	立	立	立	产	音	音	音
空	丶	八	宀	宀	穴	灾	空	空	
趣	一	十	土	扌	丰	走	走	起	起
	赿	赿	趄	趣	趣				

Unit 17, Part 1: Character Practice Sheet (Traditional Characters)

NAME _____ COURSE _____ DATE _____

壞	一	十	土	圡	坛	圹	坏	坏	埙
	埙	埙	壞	壞	壞	壞	壞	壞	壞
提	一	十	扌	扌	护	护	担	担	提
	提	提							
際	㇆	了	阝	阝	阶	阶	阶	阵	際
	際	際	際	際					
音	丶	亠	亠	立	立	产	音	音	音
空	丶	八	宀	宀	空	空	空	空	
趣	一	十	土	丰	丰	走	走	起	起
	起	起	趣	趣	趣				

Unit 17, Part 2: Character Practice Sheet (Simplified Characters)

NAME _____   COURSE _____   DATE _____

占	丶	卜	卜	占	占			
线	㇈	纟	纟	纟	纟	线	线	线
告	丿	𠂉	牛	生	牛	告	告	
诉	丶	讠	讠	诉	诉	诉	诉	
挂	一	𠂇	扌	扩	扩	护	挂	挂
传	丿	亻	亻	仁	仁	传	传	

Unit 17, Part 2: Character Practice Sheet (Traditional Characters)

NAME _____ COURSE _____ DATE _____

佔	ノ	イ	什	什	作	佔	佔		
線	ㄥ	ㄠ	幺	幺	糸	糸	糸	紒	紵
	絪	紵	綧	線	線				
告	ノ	ト	ㅛ	生	牛	告	告		
訴	ヽ	亠	亠	言	言	言	言	訂	訢
	訢	訴							
掛	一	十	扌	扩	扩	拦	拝	挂	掛
	掛								
傳	ノ	イ	仁	仁	佴	佰	佰	値	値
	傳	傳	傳						

Unit 17, Part 3: Character Practice Sheet (Simplified Characters)

NAME _____ COURSE _____ DATE _____

声	一	十	士	吉	吉	声	声		
立	丶	亠	六	立	立				
红	乙	纟	纟	纟	红	红			
黄	一	十	艹	艹	芒	苦	苦	苗	黄
黄									
图	丨	冂	冂	夕	冈	图	图	图	
领	丿	人	今	今	令	令	令	领	领
领									

Unit 17, Part 3: Character Practice Sheet (Traditional Characters)

NAME _____ COURSE _____ DATE _____

聲	一	十	士	吉	吉	吉	声	声'	声	殸
	殸	殸	聲	聲	聲	聲	聲			
立	丶	亠	宀	立	立					
紅	乙	幺	幺	幺	糸	糸	糸	紅	紅	
黃	一	十	卄	廿	芏	芇	苦	苦	苗	苗
	黃	黃								
圖	一	冂	門	門	冋	冋	冐	咼	咼	
	咼	咼	啚	圖						
領	丿	人	今	今	令	令	刟	刟	領	
	領	領	領	領						

Unit 17, Part 4: Character Practice Sheet (Simplified Characters)

NAME _____   COURSE _____   DATE _____

床	丶	一	广	广	庁	床	床		
另	丨	冂	口	马	另				
怕	丶	八	忄	忄	忄	忄	怕	怕	
树	一	十	才	木	杧	权	杈	树	树
花	一	十	艹	艻	荘	花	花		
草	一	十	艹	艹	苪	苩	苩	苩	草

Unit 17, Part 4: Character Practice Sheet (Traditional Characters)

NAME _____   COURSE _____   DATE _____

床	、	一	广	广	庄	床	床		
另	、	口	口	号	另				
怕	、	丨	忄	忄	忄	怕	怕	怕	
樹	一	十	才	木	杧	村	枯	村	桔
	桔	桔	梧	梧	樹	樹			
花	、	十	艹	艹	艾	芢	芢	花	
草	、	十	艹	艹	艹	芍	苩	苩	苷	草

Unit 18, Part 1: Character Practice Sheet (Simplified Characters)

NAME _____ COURSE _____ DATE _____

孩	ㄱ	了	子	孑	孖	孙	孩	孩	
马	ㄱ	马	马						
相	一	十	才	木	机	机	相	相	
管	ノ	ヶ	ᅑ	刋	竹	竹	竹	竹	竿
	筂	笁	管	管					
严	一	丆	ㅠ	严	严	严	严		
重	一	二	千	千	舌	盲	重	重	重

Unit 18, Part 1: Character Practice Sheet (Traditional Characters)

NAME _____ COURSE _____ DATE _____

孩	フ	了	孑	孑	孖	孖	孩	孩	孩
馬	I	厂	厂	厍	馬	馬	馬	馬	馬
相	一	十	才	木	机	村	相	相	相
管	ノ	ヶ	久	从	竹	竹	竺	竺	竿	竿
	竿	竿	管	管					
嚴	丶	口	口	叫	叩	吅	严	嚴	嚴	嚴
	严	严	屑	屑	屑	屑	嚴	嚴	嚴	嚴
重	丿	一	千	台	台	台	重	重	重

Unit 18, Part 2: Character Practice Sheet (Simplified Characters)

NAME _____   COURSE _____   DATE _____

谈	丶	讠	讠	讠	讱	谈	谈	谈	谈	谈
既	丁	刁	ヨ	刍	皀	皀	既	既	既	
送	丶	丷	丷	丷	关	关	关	送	送	
使	丿	亻	亻	仁	佢	佢	使	使		
希	丿	乂	丷	关	关	希	希			
望	丶	亠	亡	切	切	胡	胡	望	望	望
	望									

Unit 18, Part 2: Character Practice Sheet (Traditional Characters)

NAME _____ COURSE _____ DATE _____

談	丶	亠	二	言	言	言	言	言	計	訬
	訬	談	談	談	談					
既	フ	ㄱ	ㅋ	皀	皀	皀	既	既	既	
送	丶	丷	丷	丷	羊	关	关	送	送	送
使	ノ	亻	亻	亻	�乍	佇	伊	使		
希	ノ	乂	二	产	产	希	希			
望	丶	亠	亡	亡	切	切	望	望	望	望
	望									

Unit 18, Part 3: Character Practice Sheet (Simplified Characters)

NAME _____ COURSE _____ DATE _____

抽	一	十	扌	扣	扣	扣	抽	抽
烟	丶	丷	少	火	灯	灯	炉	炉	烟	烟
吸	丨	冂	口	叨	吸	吸		
区	一	フ	又	区				
情	丶	丷	忄	忄	忄	忄	忄	情	情	情
情								
帮	一	二	三	丰	邦	邦	邦	帮	帮

Unit 18, Part 3: Character Practice Sheet (Traditional Characters)

NAME _____ COURSE _____ DATE _____

| 抽 | 一 | 十 | 扌 | 打 | 扣 | 扣 | 抽 | 抽 | | |
| | | | | | | | | | | |

| 煙 | 丶 | 丷 | 少 | 火 | 灯 | 灯 | 炉 | 炳 | 炳 | 烟 |
| | 烟 | 煙 | 煙 | | | | | | | |

| 吸 | 丨 | 口 | 口 | 叮 | 叨 | 吸 | 吸 | | | |
| | | | | | | | | | | |

| 區 | 一 | 丆 | 帀 | 帀 | 品 | 品 | 品 | 品 | 品 | 品 |
| | 區 | | | | | | | | | |

| 情 | 丶 | 丨 | 忄 | 忄 | 忄 | 忕 | 忴 | 情 | 情 | 情 |
| | 情 | | | | | | | | | |

| 幫 | 一 | 十 | 土 | 圭 | 丰 | 圭 | 封 | 封 | 封 | 封 |
| | 封 | 幇 | 幇 | 幫 | 幫 | 幫 | 幫 | | | |

Unit 18, Part 4: Character Practice Sheet (Simplified Characters)

NAME _____ COURSE _____ DATE _____

容	丶	八	宀	宀	穴	灾	突	突	容	容
易	一	冂	日	日	尸	昮	昮	易		
尽	フ	ユ	尸	尺	尺	尽				
力	フ	力								
化	丿	亻	亻	化						
流	丶	冫	氵	氵	沪	浐	浐	浐	流	流

Unit 18, Part 4: Character Practice Sheet (Traditional Characters)

NAME _____   COURSE _____   DATE _____

容	丶	丷	宀	宀	穴	灾	突	突	容	容
易	一	冂	日	日	尸	吊	易	易		
盡	丁	刁	彐	圭	聿	聿	聿	聿	聿	
	書	壽	壽	盡						
力	丁	力								
化	丿	亻	仁	化						
流	丶	丶	氵	氵	泛	泛	泛	流	流	

Unit 19, Part 1: Character Practice Sheet (Simplified Characters)

NAME _____   COURSE _____   DATE _____

考	一	十	土	耂	耂	考			
试	丶	讠	讠	订	订	讠	试	试	
病	丶	亠	广	广	疒	疒	疒	病	病	病
跑	丨	冂	口	足	足	足	足	趵	趵	跑
趵	跑								
飞	乁	飞	飞						
船	丶	丿	凢	舟	舟	舟	船	船	船
船									

Unit 19, Part 1: Character Practice Sheet (Traditional Characters)

NAME _____ COURSE _____ DATE _____

考	一 十 土 耂 耂 考	
試	丶 亠 二 亖 言 言 訁 訁 訁 訁 試 試	
病	丶 亠 广 广 疒 疒 病 病 病	
跑	丶 口 口 尸 足 足 足 趵 跑 跑 跑	
飛	乀 飞 飞 飞 飛 飛 飛 飛 飛	
船	丿 丿 几 凢 舟 舟 舟 船 船 船 船	

Unit 19, Part 2: Character Practice Sheet (Simplified Characters)

NAME _____ COURSE _____ DATE _____

身	′	′	冂	甶	身	身			
体	′	′	仁	什	什	休	体		
绩	′	乡	纟	红	纩	纬	绩	绩	绩
绩									
注	′	冫	氵	沪	氵	沪	注	注	
于	一	二	于						
论	′	讠	讠	论	论	论			

Unit 19, Part 2: Character Practice Sheet (Traditional Characters)

NAME _____ COURSE _____ DATE _____

身	⟍	⼈	⼓	甶	皀	身	身		

體	⼁	⼌	冎	冎	咼	丹	骨	骨	骨
骨	骭	骬	骮	骭	骲	骳	骴	骵	骶
骹	髎	體							

績	⼃	⼥	幺	糸	糸	糸	紅	紶	結	結
結	結	績	績	績	績	績				

注	⟍	⼆	⼺	氵	汀	汻	汢	注		

於	⟍	⼇	方	方	扗	於	於			

論	⟍	⼇	亠	言	言	言	訁	訡	訡	
訡	論	論	論	論						

Unit 19, Part 3: Character Practice Sheet (Simplified Characters)

NAME _____ COURSE _____ DATE _____

向	′	′	冂	囱	向	向				
眼	⏐	冂	刀	月	目	目˥	目⁊	目⁊	眼	眼
	眼									
连	一	左	左	车	车	连	连			
利	′	⁓	千	千	禾	利	利			
产	′	一	亠	六	立	产				
义	′	丷	义							

Unit 19, Part 3: Character Practice Sheet (Traditional Characters)

NAME _____ COURSE _____ DATE _____

向	㇆	亻	冂	向	向	向		

眼	丨	冂	月	月	目	目	目	目	眼	眼
眼										

連	一	厂	冂	百	百	亘	車	車	連	連
連										

利	ノ	二	千	千	禾	利	利		

產	丶	二	亠	文	立	产	产	产	彦	產
產										

義	丶	丷	꼭	꼭	⺷	羊	羊	羊	羊	羊
義	義	義								

Unit 19, Part 4: Character Practice Sheet (Simplified Characters)

NAME _____　COURSE _____　DATE _____

责	一	二	丰	圭	责	青	责	责
任	丿	亻	亻	仁	仁	仟	任	
父	丿	八	少	父				
母	ㄴ	ㄑ	母	母	母			
教	一	十	土	耂	耂	孝	孝	教 教
	教							
信	丿	亻	亻	广	作	信	信	信

Unit 19, Part 4: Character Practice Sheet (Traditional Characters)

NAME _____   COURSE _____   DATE _____

責	一	二	丰	主	青	青	青	青	青	責
	責									
任	ノ	イ	仁	仁	仟	任				
父	ノ	ハ	父	父						
母	ㄥ	母	母	母	母					
教	一	十	土	耂	考	考	孝	孝	教	教
	教									
信	ノ	イ	仁	仁	作	作	信	信	信	信

Unit 20, Part 1: Character Practice Sheet (Simplified Characters)

NAME _____   COURSE _____   DATE _____

唱	丨	冂	口	口丿	口冂	口門	口昌	叩	唱	唱
	唱								
歌	一	丁	可	可	可	可	哥	哥	哥	哥
	哥	歌	歌	歌					
怪	丶	八	忄	忄	忄	怪	怪	怪		
观	フ	又	刈	观	观	观				
画	一	丆	币	両	両	画	画			
照	丨	冂	日	日	日フ	日刀	日刀	昭	昭	昭
	照	照	照						

Unit 20, Part 1: Character Practice Sheet (Traditional Characters)

NAME _____ COURSE _____ DATE _____

唱	丶	丷	口	叮	叮	叮	唱	唱	唱	唱
	唱								
歌	一	一	丆	可	可	可	哥	哥	哥	哥
	哥	歌	歌	歌					
怪	丶	丨	忄	忄	忸	怪	怪	怪		
觀	丶	艹	艹	艹	苩	苩	苩	茁	茁	茁
	茁	莭	莭	華	華	雚	雚	雚	雚	雚
	雚	觀	觀	觀	觀				
畫	一	冖	尹	聿	聿	聿	書	書	書	畵
	畫	畫							
照	丨	冂	日	日	日ㄅ	昭	昭	昭	昭	昭
	照	照	照						

Unit 20, Part 2: Character Practice Sheet (Simplified Characters)

NAME _____ COURSE _____ DATE _____

研	一	ㄧ	石	石	石	石	矴	研	研	
究	、	ㄴ	宀	宀	穴	穷	究			
懂	丶	丷	忄	忄	忄	忄	忄	怑	怑	惛
	惛	惛	懂	懂	懂					
民	ㄱ	ㄱ	𡚝	民	民					
华	ノ	イ	化	化	华	华				
亲	丶	亠	立	立	立	辛	辛	亲	亲	

Unit 20, Part 2: Character Practice Sheet (Traditional Characters)

NAME _____ COURSE _____ DATE _____

研	一	丆	不	石	石	石一	石二	矵	研
究	、	八	宀	宀	空	究	究		
懂	、	忄	忄	忄	忄	忄一	忄艹	忄芏	忄苎	忄惜
	惜	惜	惜	懂	懂	懂			
民	フ	ㄱ	尸	尸	民	民			
華	、	十	十一	艹	芏	芏	莘	莘	華
	華	華							
親	、	二	立	立	立	立	辛	亲	亲	亲刂
	亲刂	新	亲刂	親	親	親			

Unit 20, Part 3: Character Practice Sheet (Simplified Characters)

NAME _____   COURSE _____   DATE _____

影	丨	冂	曰	日	旦	昱	早	昺	景	景
	景	景	影	影	影					
新	丶	亠	亠	立	立	辛	亲	亲	亲	
	新	新	新							
故	一	十	古	古	古	故	故	故		
将	丶	丬	丬	爿	将	将	将	将	将	
计	丶	讠	计	计						
划	一	七	戈	戈	划	划				

Unit 20, Part 3: Character Practice Sheet (Traditional Characters)

NAME _____ COURSE _____ DATE _____

影	、	冂	日	日	早	县	早	景	景	景
	景	景	景	影	影					

新	、	亠	立	立	立	立	辛	辛	亲	亲
	新	新	新							

故	一	十	十	古	古	古	古	故	故	

將	㇀	㇇	爿	爿	爿	狀	將	將	將	將
	將									

計	、	亠	亠	言	言	言	言	計	計	

劃	㇆	㇇	�글	글	聿	聿	書	書	書	畵
	書	畫	畫	劃						

Unit 20, Part 4: Character Practice Sheet (Simplified Characters)

NAME _____   COURSE _____   DATE _____

类	丶	丷	丷	半	米	米	类	类	类
排	一	十	扌	扫	打	排	排	排	排	排
	排								
楼	一	十	才	木	栏	栏	栏	栌	梻	楼
	栌	楼	楼						
部	丶	二	六	立	立	产	音	音	咅	部
理	一	二	王	王	玑	珇	珇	珇	理	理
	理								
它	丶	丷	宀	宀	它				

Unit 20, Part 4: Character Practice Sheet (Traditional Characters)

NAME _____   COURSE _____   DATE _____

類	丶	⺀	⺌	半	米	米	类	类	类	类
	类	类	类	类	類	類	類	類	類	

| 排 | 一 | 十 | 扌 | 扌 | 扪 | 扫 | 排 | 排 | 排 | 排 |
| | 排 | | | | | | | | | |

| 樓 | 一 | 十 | 才 | 木 | 杧 | 杧 | 桴 | 桙 | 桙 | 桙 |
| | 桙 | 樓 | 樓 | 樓 | 樓 | | | | | |

部	丶	一	十	立	立	产	音	音	音	音
	部									

| 理 | 一 | 二 | 千 | 王 | 玏 | 玣 | 玶 | 理 | 理 | 理 |
| | 理 | | | | | | | | | |

它	丶	宀	宀	宀	它					

Unit 21, Part 1: Character Practice Sheet (Simplified Characters)

NAME _____ COURSE _____ DATE _____

球	一	二	于	王	王	玎	玎	珄	球
	球								
队	了	阝	阞	队					
运	一	二	云	云	运	运	运		
功	一	丁	工	巧	功				
室	、	丷	宀	宀	宏	宏	宏	室	室
倒	丿	亻	亻	亻	仁	伍	侄	倒	倒

Unit 21, Part 1: Character Practice Sheet (Traditional Characters)

NAME _____　COURSE _____　DATE _____

球	一	二	干	王	王	求	求	求	球
	球								
隊	フ	㇏	阝	阝	阝	阝	阝	阼	隊
	隊	隊							
運	丶	冖	冖	尸	злал	злал	冒	宣	軍
	軍	渾	運						
功	一	丁	工	巧	功				
室	丶	丷	宀	宀	宏	宏	宰	室	
倒	丿	亻	仁	仁	仵	侄	侄	倒	倒

Unit 21, Part 2: Character Practice Sheet (Simplified Characters)

NAME ______________________ COURSE ______________________ DATE ______________________

假
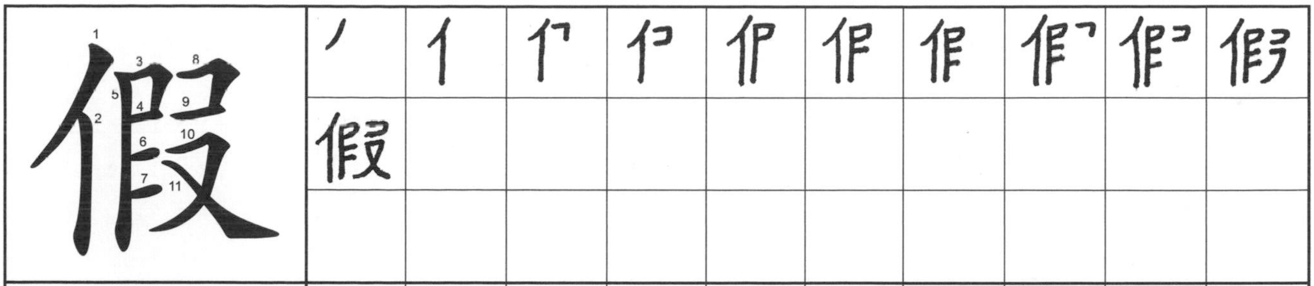

春
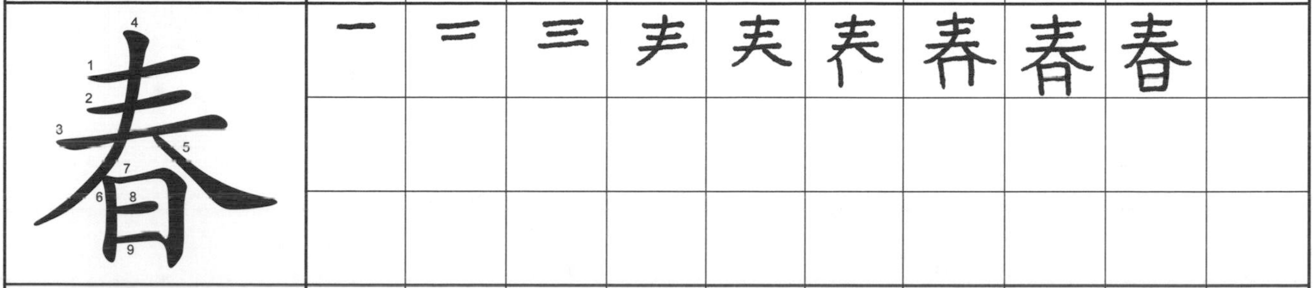

整
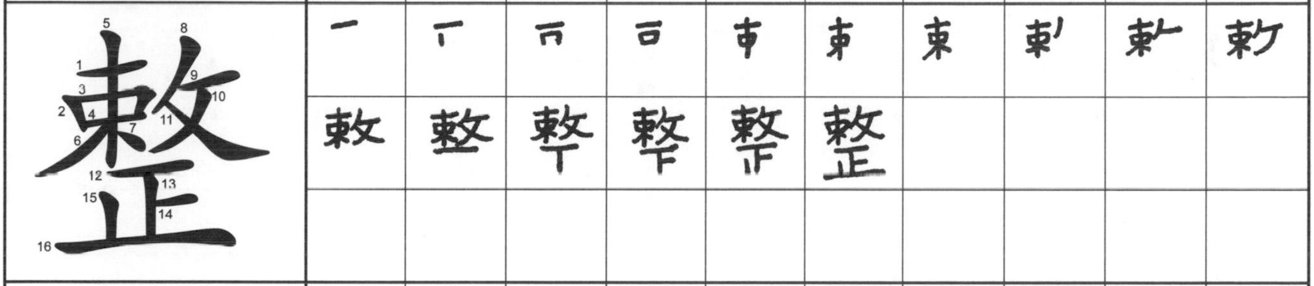

育
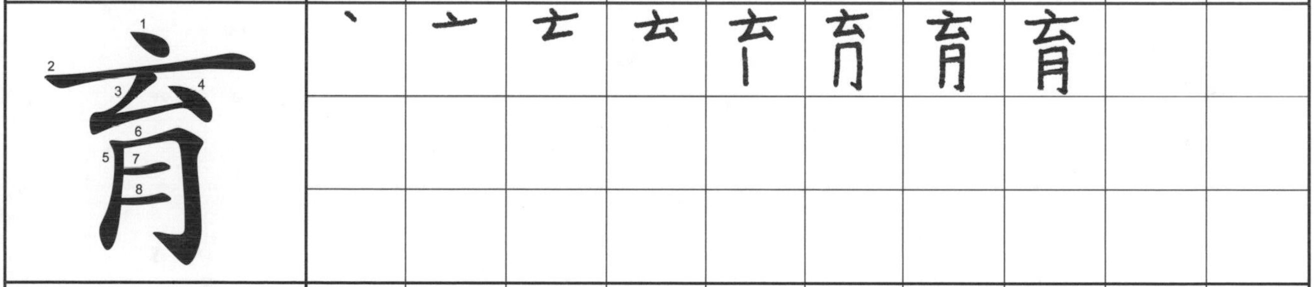

社
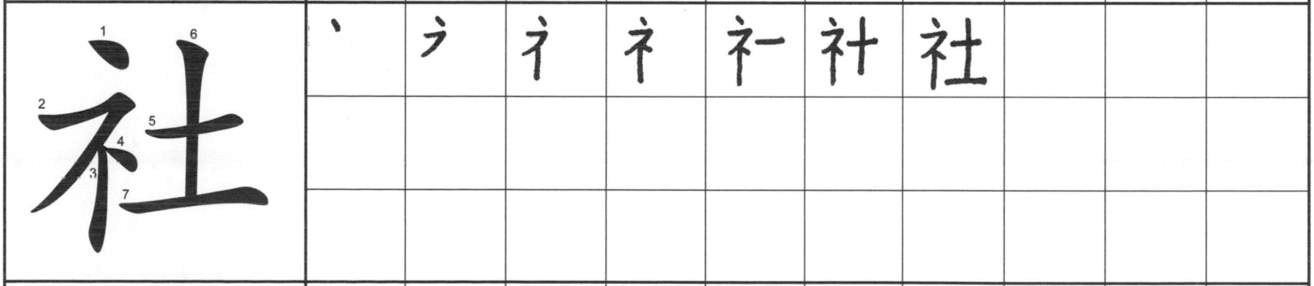

团

Unit 21, Part 2: Character Practice Sheet (Traditional Characters)

NAME _____ COURSE _____ DATE _____

假	ノ	イ	仃	仃	仴	作	作	作	作	假
	假									
春	一	二	三	夫	夫	表	春	春	春	
整	一	一	一	曰	中	申	束	剌	敕	敕
	敕	敕	整	整	整	整				
育	一	亡	女	方	育	育	育			
社	丶	㇀	ネ	ネ	社	社	社			
團	丨	冂	冂	冃	同	同	同	團	團	團
	團	團	團	團						

Unit 21, Part 3: Character Practice Sheet (Simplified Characters)

NAME _____ COURSE _____ DATE _____

世	一	十	卅	廿	世				
界	丨	冂	日	用	田	罘	罘	界	界
目	丨	冂	月	目	目				
视	丶	礻	礻	礻	衤	初	初	视	
强	フ	ユ	弓	引	弔	弔	弔	弘	弜	强
	强	强							
足	丶	冂	口	모	무	무	足	足	

Unit 21, Part 3: Character Practice Sheet (Traditional Characters)

NAME _____   COURSE _____   DATE _____

世	一	十	廿	世	世				
界	丨	冂	口	田	田	甼	界	界	界
目	丨	冂	月	月	目				
視	丶	礻	礻	礻	礽	初	視	祖	祖
	視								
強	乛	弓	弓	弘	弘	弘	強	強	強
	強								
足	丶	冂	口	甲	卩	足	足		

Unit 21, Part 4: Character Practice Sheet (Simplified Characters)

NAME _____ COURSE _____ DATE _____

	底	、	亠	广	广	庀	庍	底	底		
	建	⁊	⁊	⁊	⁊	彐	聿	建	建		
	修	⁊	亻	亻	亻	伫	修	修	修	修	
	靠	⁊	⁻	⁺	生	牛	告	告	告	靠	
		靠	靠	靠	靠	靠					
	战	⁊	⁐	⁺	占	占	占	战	战	战	
	争	⁊	⁊	刍	刍	刍	争				

Unit 21, Part 4: Character Practice Sheet (Traditional Characters)

NAME _____   COURSE _____   DATE _____

底	丶	宀	广	庐	庐	庍	底	底		
建	乛	彐	彐	彐	彐	聿	津	律	建	
修	丿	亻	亻	伬	伬	攸	攸	修	修	修
靠	丶	亠	屮	生	牛	告	告	告	告	告
	告	告	靠	靠	靠					
戰	丶	冂	口	吅	吅	吅	吅	吅	昍	單
	單	單	單	戰	戰	戰				
爭	丿	丷	爫	爫	爭	爭	爭	爭		

Unit 22, Part 1: Character Practice Sheet (Simplified Characters)

NAME _____　COURSE _____　DATE _____

医	一	丆	芣	玉	至	医	医		
院	了	阝	阝	阝	陀	陀	陀	阼	院
变	丶	亠	十	亣	亦	亦	变	变	
许	丶	讠	讠	讣	许	许			
志	一	十	士	志	志	志	志		
英	一	十	艹	艹	芇	苂	荚	英	

Unit 22, Part 1: Character Practice Sheet (Traditional Characters)

NAME _____ COURSE _____ DATE _____

醫	一	丁	匚	丟	医	医	医	医	医殳
	医殳	医殳	醫	醫	醫	醫	醫	醫	
院	フ	了	阝	阝'	阝`	阺	阼	陀	陀	院
變	丶	亠	亠	言	言	言	言	信	絲	結
	結	結	結	結	絲	絲	絲	絲	絲	絲
	戀	變	變						
許	丶	亠	亠	言	言	言	言	訂	訐	許
	許								
志	一	十	士	亠	志	志	志		
英	丶	十	廾	艹	艹	苎	苙	英	英

Unit 22, Part 2: Character Practice Sheet (Simplified Characters)

NAME _____ COURSE _____ DATE _____

偷	′	亻	亻	亻	价	价	偷	偷	偷
	偷								
赶	一	十	土	丰	丰	走	走	赶	赶
读	`	讠	讠	讠	读	读	读	读	读
护	一	十	扌	扩	护	护	护		
皮	﹁	厂	广	皮	皮				
被	`	讠	礻	礻	衤	衫	被	被	被

Unit 22, Part 2: Character Practice Sheet (Traditional Characters)

NAME _____ COURSE _____ DATE _____

偷	ノ	ノ	亻	俨	俨	价	俞	俞	俞	偷
	偷									
趕	一	十	土	圥	走	走	走	走	赵	起
	趕	趕	趕	趕						
讀	丶	亠	亖	言	言	言	言	言	計	詰
	訃	讀	讀	讀	讀	讀	讀	讀	讀	讀
	讀	讀								
護	丶	亠	亖	言	言	言	計	言	計	許
	誜	誜	許	許	許	諎	護	護	護	護
	護									
皮	一	厂	广	皮	皮					
被	丶	丆	礻	礻	礻	礽	衸	衪	衵	被

Unit 22, Part 3: Character Practice Sheet (Simplified Characters)

NAME _____   COURSE _____   DATE _____

掉	一	十	扌	扩	护	扣	护	抖	掉
	掉								
火	`	``	少	火					
检	一	十	才	木	术	朴	检	检	检	检
	检									
查	一	十	十	木	术	查	杏	杳	查
危	`	勹	匕	产	夯	危			
险	了	阝	阝	阶	险	险	险	险	

Unit 22, Part 3: Character Practice Sheet (Traditional Characters)

NAME _____ COURSE _____ DATE _____

掉	一	寸	扌	扩	扩	扩	护	掉	掉
	掉								
火	丶	ヽ	少	火					
檢	一	十	才	木	朼	朴	栓	栓	栓	栓
	检	梌	梌	梌	檢	檢	檢			
查	一	十	才	木	木	杏	杏	查	查
危	ノ	ク	勹	产	乃	危			
險	ヽ	了	阝	阝	队	阶	险	险	险
	阶	险	险	险	险	險			

Unit 22, Part 4: Character Practice Sheet (Simplified Characters)

NAME _____   COURSE _____   DATE _____

伤	丿	亻	亻	仵	仿	伤				
破	一	丆	丆	石	石	矿	矿	矿	砣	破
结	乚	乡	纟	纟	纴	纴	绀	结	结	
发	乛	乜	发	发	发					
费	一	一	弓	弓	弗	弗	弗	费	费	
合	丿	人	人	今	合	合				

Unit 22, Part 4: Character Practice Sheet (Traditional Characters)

NAME _____ COURSE _____ DATE _____

傷	ノ	ノ	イ	イ	广	竹	佇	佰	佰	侮	傷
	傷	傷	傷								
破	一	丁	石	石	石	矴	矿	砂	破	破	
結	ㄥ	幺	幺	糸	糸	糸	紀	紒	結	結	
	結	結									
發	フ	ㄢ	癶	癶	癶	癶	癶	發	發	發	
	發	發									
費	一	二	弓	弗	弗	弗	弗	費	費	費	
	費	費									
合	ノ	人	仝	合	合	合					

Unit 23, Part 1: Character Practice Sheet (Simplified Characters)

NAME _____ COURSE _____ DATE _____

指	一	寸	扌	扩	扗	拤	指	指	指	
导	⌐	⊃	巳	豆	导	导				
组	ㄥ	ㄥ	ㄠ	纟	纠	织	纽	组	组	
并	丶	ﾉﾉ	ㅗㅗ	兰	兰	并	并			
济	丶	冫	氵	氵	汇	沪	汶	济	济	
制	ﾉ	ﾄ	ㅏ	乍	告	制	制	制		

Unit 23, Part 1: Character Practice Sheet (Traditional Characters)

NAME ______________________ COURSE ______________________ DATE ______________________

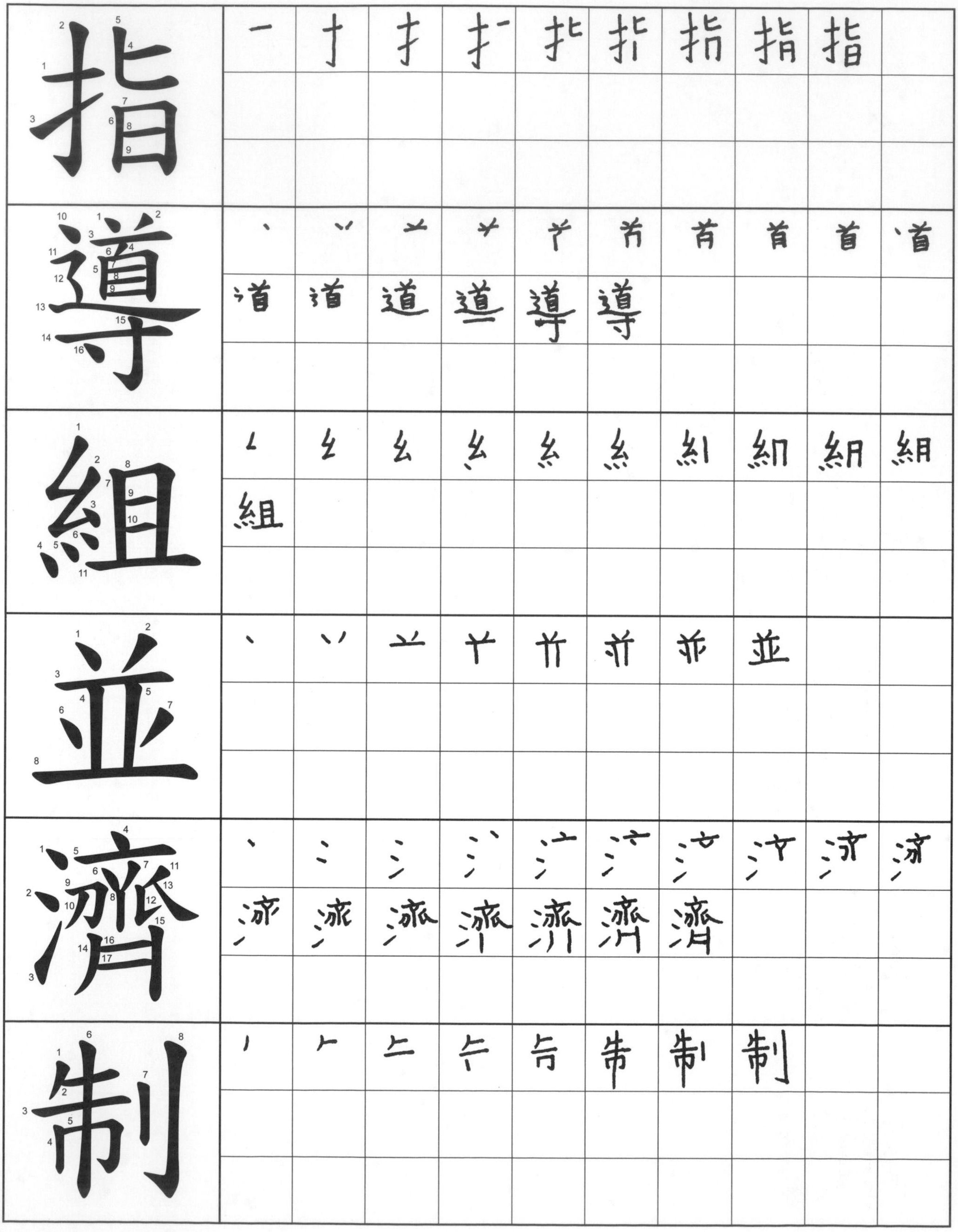

Unit 23, Part 2: Character Practice Sheet (Simplified Characters)

NAME _____   COURSE _____   DATE _____

银	ノ	卜	卢	钅	钅	钌	钌	钌	银	银
	银								
存	一	ナ	才	存	存	存			
统	ㄥ	纟	纟	纟	纟	纩	纩	纩	统
般	′	ノ	几	舟	舟	舟	舟′	舟′	船	般
商	丶	一	亠	产	产	商	商	商	商
	商								
光	ノ	丷	丷	业	光	光			

Unit 23, Part 2: Character Practice Sheet (Traditional Characters)

NAME _____ COURSE _____ DATE _____

銀	ノ	㇀	㇒	亼	숃	숙	金	金	金丁	金ㄱ
	釒ㄱ	釖	銀	銀						
存	一	广	才	存	存	存				
統	㇀	幺	幺	糸	糸	糸	糸	統	統	紡
	統									
般	㇀	ノ	丹	月	舟	舟	舟'	舟几	舟几	般
商	丶	亠	古	产	产	产	芮	商	商	
	商									
光	㇑	业	业	业	半	光				

Unit 23, Part 3: Character Practice Sheet (Simplified Characters)

NAME _____ COURSE _____ DATE _____

官	、	ハ	宀	宀	宁	宁	官	官		

| 普 | 、 | ソ | ソ | ソ | 並 | 艹 | 並 | 並 | 普 | 普 |
| | 普 | 普 | | | | | | | | |

| 政 | 一 | T | F | 正 | 正 | 正 | 政 | 政 | 政 | |
| | | | | | | | | | | |

| 策 | ノ | 广 | 广 | ⺮ | ⺮ | ⺮ | 竺 | 竺 | 竺 | 第 |
| | 第 | 策 | | | | | | | | |

| 基 | 一 | 十 | 廿 | 廿 | 甘 | 其 | 其 | 其 | 其 | 基 |
| | 基 | | | | | | | | | |

周	ノ	几	月	用	用	周	周			

Unit 23, Part 3: Character Practice Sheet (Traditional Characters)

NAME _____ COURSE _____ DATE _____

官	丶	八	宀	宀	宁	宁	官	官		
普	丶	丷	坐	并	並	並	並	並	普	普
	普	普								
政	一	丁	下	正	正	正	政	政	政	
策	丿	𠂆	乍	竹	竹	竹	竹	竻	筞	策
	策	策								
基	一	十	廿	甘	甘	其	其	其	其	基
	基									
週	丿	冂	月	円	用	用	周	周	周	週
	週	週								

Unit 23, Part 4: Character Practice Sheet (Simplified Characters)

NAME _____ COURSE _____ DATE _____

迎	′	﹂	幻	卬	卬	迎	迎
历	一	厂	历	历			
史	′	冂	口	史	史		
式	一	二	于	王	式	式	
达	一	才	大	大	达	达	
府	′	一	广	广	庁	府	府	府

Unit 23, Part 4: Character Practice Sheet (Traditional Characters)

NAME _____ COURSE _____ DATE _____

迎	╱	⺅	⼄	印	⼱	迎	迎	迎	
歷	一	厂	厂	厂	厈	厈	厤	厤	厤
	厤	麻	歷	歷	歷	歷			
史	╲	冂	口	史	史				
式	一	二	丁	王	式	式			
達	一	十	土	圡	去	去	查	幸	幸
	達	達	達						
府	╲	亠	广	广	庁	府	府		

Unit 24, Part 1: Character Practice Sheet (Simplified Characters)

NAME _____　COURSE _____　DATE _____

据	一	亅	扌	扩	护	护	护	护	据
	据								
创	丿	人	仒	仓	创	创			
约	乚	纟	纟	丝	约	约			
至	一	工	云	至	至	至			
此	丨	止	止	此	此	此			
响	丨	冂	口	叮	叮	响	响	响	响

Unit 24, Part 1: Character Practice Sheet (Traditional Characters)

NAME _____ COURSE _____ DATE _____

| 據 | 一 | 十 | 才 | 扩 | 扩 | 扩 | 护 | 护 | 护 | 掳 |
| | 据 | 据 | 据 | 据 | 據 | 據 | | | | |

| 創 | ノ | 人 | 仝 | 今 | 今 | 今 | 倉 | 倉 | 倉 | 倉 |
| | 倉 | 創 | | | | | | | | |

約	㇍	幺	幺	糸	糸	糸	糸	約	約	

至	一	乙	云	互	至	至				

此	㇑	𠂆	止	止	此	此				

響	㇀	幺	乡	乡	纟	纟	纟	纟	纟	纟
	纟ß	鄉	鄉	鄉	響	響	響	響	響	響
	響									

Unit 24, Part 2: Character Practice Sheet (Simplified Characters)

NAME _____   COURSE _____   DATE _____

虎	✓	⼘	卢	卢	卢	虍	虏	虎	
环	一	二	干	王	环	环	环	环	
境	一	十	土	圹	圹	圹	圹	垃	培
	垆	垆	境	境					
断	、	✓	丷	半	米	米	迷	迷	断
	断								
绝	✓	⺰	纟	纟	纟	纟	绝	绝	绝
奶	✓	女	女	奶	奶				

Unit 24, Part 2: Character Practice Sheet (Traditional Characters)

NAME _____ COURSE _____ DATE _____

虎	㇑	㇏	上	虍	虍	虍	虍	虎	
環	一	二	王	王	玉	玕	珇	玛	珢
	珢	珢	珢	珢	環	環	環		
境	一	十	土	圡	圹	圹	圹	垃	培
	培	培	塄	境					
斷	㇀	幺	幺	幺	絲	絲	絲	燊	䇠	䇠
	䇠	䇠	絲	㡭	斷	斷	斷	斷	
絕	㇀	幺	幺	幺	糸	糸	糾	糾	紹	紹
	紹	絕							
奶	㇑	女	女	妁	奶				

Unit 24, Part 3: Character Practice Sheet (Simplified Characters)

NAME _____   COURSE _____   DATE _____

独	ノ	犭	犭	犭	狆	独	独	独	
科	一	二	千	禾	禾	禾	科	科	
收	し	丩	丩	収	収	收			
缺	ノ	午	午	午	缶	缶	缶	缺	缺
律	ノ	彳	彳	彳	彳	律	律	律	
印	ノ	匚	匚	印	印				

Unit 24, Part 3: Character Practice Sheet (Traditional Characters)

NAME _____ COURSE _____ DATE _____

獨	´	㇈	犭	犭	狆	犭	犭	犭	犭
	犸	獨	獨	獨	獨	獨			
科	´	㇒	千	千	禾	禾	秆	秆	科
收	㇄	㇇	屮	屮	収	收			
缺	´	㇀	二	午	缶	缶	缶	缺	缺
律	´	㇒	彳	彳	彳	伊	律	律	律
印	´	㇒	千	臣	臼	印			

Unit 24, Part 4: Character Practice Sheet (Simplified Characters)

NAME _____ COURSE _____ DATE _____

型	一	二	千	开	刑	刑	型	型	型
脑	丿	刀	月	月	月`	脌	肟	胶	脑	脑
无	一	二	于	无					
网	丨	冂	冂	网	网	网			
装	丶	丬	爿	壮	壮	壮	壮	装	裝
	装	装							
造	丿	丿	丬	生	牛	告	告	造	造

Unit 24, Part 4: Character Practice Sheet (Traditional Characters)

NAME _____   COURSE _____   DATE _____

型	一	二	于	开	刑	刑	刑	型
腦	丿	刀	月	月	肋	肌	胏	腦
腦	腦	腦						
無	丿	仁	上	午	缶	無	無	無
無	無							
網	乙	幺	幺	糸	糸	糸	紆	紉	網
網	網	網	網					
裝	乚	丩	爿	爿	壯	壯	壯	裝
裝	裝	裝						
造	丿	牛	牛	告	告	造	造	造
造								

Reading and Writing Exercises for *Intermediate Written Chinese* Lessons 11-1 to 24-4

Reading and Writing Exercises for IWC Lesson 11-1

NAME _____ COURSE _____ DATE _____

A. Transcribe what you hear on the accompanying audio disc into Chinese characters.

(1)

(2)

(3)

B. If a reference is given after a question, answer based on the referenced part of the Reading Exercises. If no reference is indicated, you may answer any way you wish.

(1) 司机为什么说"没问题，你放心吧"？
(司機為什麼說"沒問題，你放心吧"？) B1

(2) 那个人觉得要决定的事，得怎么样？
(那個人覺得要決定的事，得怎麼樣？) C

(3) 你开车开得快不快？慢不慢？(你開車開得快不快？慢不慢？)

(4) 你最近有没有什么问题需要解决？
(你最近有沒有什麼問題需要解決？)

Reading and Writing Exercises for IWC Lesson 11-2

NAME _____ COURSE _____ DATE _____

A. Transcribe what you hear on the accompanying audio disc into Chinese characters.

(1)

(2)

(3)

B. If a reference is given after a question, answer based on the referenced part of the Reading Exercises. If no reference is indicated, you may answer any way you wish.

(1) 那个老外为什么得上了公车以后再买票？
(那個老外為什麼得上了公車以後再買票？) B1

(2) 这个人知道不知道他的外国朋友现在在哪里？
(這個人知道不知道他的外國朋友現在在哪裏？) C1

(3) 请问，你去过香港或者台湾吗？
(請問，你去過香港或者台灣嗎？)

(4) 要是有一个人见到你和你说"好久不见！"，那么你应该说什么？
(要是有一個人見到你和你說"好久不見！"，那麼你應該說什麼？)

Reading and Writing Exercises for IWC Lesson 11-3

NAME _____ COURSE _____ DATE _____

A. Transcribe what you hear on the accompanying audio disc into Chinese characters.

(1)

(2)

(3)

B. If a reference is given after a question, answer based on the referenced part of the Reading Exercises. If no reference is indicated, you may answer any way you wish.

(1) 从这里去和平家具店，怎么走？
（從這裏去和平家具店，怎麼走？）B2

(2) 那个人住的房子，左手边有什么，右手边有什么？
（那個人住的房子，左手邊有什麼，右手邊有什麼？）c

(3) 你住的房间里，家具多不多？（你住的房間裏，家具多不多？）

(4) 要是有人跟你讲中国话，你一定跟他讲中国话吗？
（要是有人跟你講中國話，你一定跟他講中國話嗎？）

··

Reading and Writing Exercises for IWC Lesson 11-4

NAME _____ COURSE _____ DATE _____

A. Transcribe what you hear on the accompanying audio disc into Chinese characters.

(1)

(2)

(3)

B. If a reference is given after a question, answer based on the referenced part of the Reading Exercises. If no reference is indicated, you may answer any way you wish.

(1) 那个人为什么说以后要坐公车或者走路去上班？
   (那個人為什麼說以後要坐公車或者走路去上班？) c1

(2) 这两位大学校长要解决什么问题？
   (這兩位大學校長要解決什麼問題？) c2

(3) 在美国，什么东西价钱特别贵？
   (在美國，什麼東西價錢特別貴？)

(4) 你加油的时候，是不是一定加满？
   (你加油的時候，是不是一定加滿？)

Reading and Writing Exercises for IWC Lesson 12-1

NAME _____   COURSE _____   DATE _____

A. Transcribe what you hear on the accompanying audio disc into Chinese characters.

(1)

(2)

(3)

B. If a reference is given after a question, answer based on the referenced part of the Reading Exercises. If no reference is indicated, you may answer any way you wish.

(1) 那位女生的老师觉得加拿大的法文比较好听还是法国的法文比较好听？
(那位女生的老師覺得加拿大的法文比較好聽還是法國的法文比較好聽？) B2

(2) 请问，那个人已经知道以后要找什么样的工作了吗？
(請問，那個人已經知道以後要找什麼樣的工作了嗎？) C2

(3) 你已经决定你的专业了吗？（你已經決定你的專業了嗎？）

(4) 要是你找一个人可是他不在，你怎么办？
(要是你找一個人可是他不在，你怎麼辦？)

Reading and Writing Exercises for IWC Lesson 12-2

NAME _____   COURSE _____   DATE _____

A. Transcribe what you hear on the accompanying audio disc into Chinese characters.

(1)

(2)

(3)

B. If a reference is given after a question, answer based on the referenced part of the Reading Exercises. If no reference is indicated, you may answer any way you wish.

(1) 哪种本子好像有两百张纸？是这种还是那种？
（哪種本子好像有兩百張紙？是這種還是那種？）A9

(2) 那个人现在很想到哪儿去买什么？
（那個人現在很想到哪兒去買什麼？）C2

(3) 你正在想什么呢？（你正在想什麼呢？）

(4) 你喜欢看报纸吗？你看什么报纸？
（你喜歡看報紙嗎？你看什麼報紙？）

Reading and Writing Exercises for IWC Lesson 12-3

NAME _____   COURSE _____   DATE _____

A. Transcribe what you hear on the accompanying audio disc into Chinese characters.

(1)

(2)

(3)

B. If a reference is given after a question, answer based on the referenced part of the Reading Exercises. If no reference is indicated, you may answer any way you wish.

(1) 到了加拿大之后，"我"才知道什么？
(到了加拿大之後，"我"才知道甚麼？) A5

(2) 要是买一斤白菜，要多少钱？
(要是買一斤白菜，要多少錢？) B1

(3) 你能保证这个菜好吃吗？(你能保證這個菜好吃嗎？)

(4) 你喜欢不喜欢吃中国菜？(你喜歡不喜歡吃中國菜？)

Reading and Writing Exercises for IWC Lesson 12-4

NAME _____ COURSE _____ DATE _____

A. Transcribe what you hear on the accompanying audio disc into Chinese characters.

(1)

(2)

(3)

B. If a reference is given after a question, answer based on the referenced part of the Reading Exercises. If no reference is indicated, you may answer any way you wish.

(1) 手里拿着公事包的那位老师叫什么名字？
　　（手裏拿着公事包的那位老師叫什麼名字？）A3

(2) 那个人以后要是有钱，想吃进口的菜和进口的什么东西？
　　（那個人以後要是有錢，想吃進口的菜和進口的什麼東西？）C1

(3) 你总共会说几种语言？（你總共會說幾種語言？）

(4) 你有没有公事包？你的中文老师呢？
　　（你有沒有公事包？你的中文老師呢？）

Reading and Writing Exercises for IWC Lesson 13-1

NAME _____ COURSE _____ DATE _____

A. Transcribe what you hear on the accompanying audio disc into Chinese characters.

(1)

(2)

(3)

B. If a reference is given after a question, answer based on the referenced part of the Reading Exercises. If no reference is indicated, you may answer any way you wish.

(1) 小李现在的这个工作忙不忙？
　　(小李現在的這個工作忙不忙？) c1

(2) 为什么那个人切肉、切菜的时候，他小妹离他很远？
　　(為什麼那個人切肉、切菜的時候，他小妹離他很遠？) c2

(3) 美国的食品店卖什么？(美國的食品店賣甚麼？)

(4) 你比较喜欢吃面包跟牛肉，还是面包跟水果？
　　(你比較喜歡吃麵包跟牛肉，還是麵包跟水果？)

Reading and Writing Exercises for IWC Lesson 13-2

NAME _____ COURSE _____ DATE _____

A. Transcribe what you hear on the accompanying audio disc into Chinese characters.

(1)

(2)

(3)

B. If a reference is given after a question, answer based on the referenced part of the Reading Exercises. If no reference is indicated, you may answer any way you wish.

(1) 入口在哪儿？出口在哪儿？（入口在哪兒？出口在哪兒？）A3

(2) 那个人的弟弟、妹妹主张什么？
（那個人的弟弟、妹妹主張什麼？）A5

(3) 你很节省吗？（你很節省嗎？）

(4) 中文学起来很有意思吧？（中文學起來很有意思吧？）

Reading and Writing Exercises for IWC Lesson 13-3

NAME _____ COURSE _____ DATE _____

A. Transcribe what you hear on the accompanying audio disc into Chinese characters.

(1)

(2)

(3)

B. If a reference is given after a question, answer based on the referenced part of the Reading Exercises. If no reference is indicated, you may answer any way you wish.

(1) 那个卖鞋的为什么不能少算一点？

（那個賣鞋的為什麼不能少算一點？）B1

(2) 她们为什么决定一个人买黑色的高跟鞋，一个人买白色的高跟鞋？

（她們為什麼決定一個人買黑色的高跟鞋，一個人買白色的高跟鞋？）C1

(3) 你穿几号的鞋？（你穿幾號的鞋？）

(4) 你在你现在住的地方总共有几双鞋？

（你在你現在住的地方總共有幾雙鞋？）

Reading and Writing Exercises for IWC Lesson 13-4

NAME _____ COURSE _____ DATE _____

A. Transcribe what you hear on the accompanying audio disc into Chinese characters.

(1)

(2)

(3)

B. If a reference is given after a question, answer based on the referenced part of the Reading Exercises. If no reference is indicated, you may answer any way you wish.

(1) 年家平说他什么时候给李老师他的作业？
(年家平說他什麼時候給李老師他的作業？) B4

(2) 那个人保证下次如果还去广州的话，一定会多带一些什么？
为什么？
(那個人保證下次如果還去廣州的話，一定會多帶一些什麼？
為什麼？) C1

(3) 雨衣应该什么时候穿？（雨衣應該什麼時候穿？）

(4) 你如果需要买衣服的话，到哪儿去买？
(你如果需要買衣服的話，到哪兒去買？)

Reading and Writing Exercises for IWC Lesson 14-1

NAME _____ COURSE _____ DATE _____

A. Transcribe what you hear on the accompanying audio disc into Chinese characters.

(1)

(2)

(3)

B. If a reference is given after a question, answer based on the referenced part of the Reading Exercises. If no reference is indicated, you may answer any way you wish.

(1) 王大海是用左手写字还是用右手写字？你觉得这是为什么？
(王大海是用左手寫字還是用右手寫字？你覺得這是為什麼？)
A10

(2) 那个美国人想在哪儿吃饭？(那個美國人想在哪兒吃飯？) B1

(3) 五百块够不够你用一个月？(五百塊夠不夠你用一個月？)

(4) 你爸爸妈妈会不会说中国话？(你爸爸媽媽會不會說中國話？)

Reading and Writing Exercises for IWC Lesson 14-2

NAME _____ COURSE _____ DATE _____

A. Transcribe what you hear on the accompanying audio disc into Chinese characters.

(1)

(2)

(3)

B. If a reference is given after a question, answer based on the referenced part of the Reading Exercises. If no reference is indicated, you may answer any way you wish.

(1) 你觉得，金小姐跟李先生大概是什么关系？
(你覺得，金小姐跟李先生大概是甚麼關係？) A8

(2) 小李为什么不能吃了饭再走？
(小李為什麼不能吃了飯再走？) B2

(3) 您喜欢喝酒吗？(您喜歡喝酒嗎？)

(4) 你如果有一天没有米饭吃，你受得了吗？
(你如果有一天沒有米飯吃，你受得了嗎？)

Reading and Writing Exercises for IWC Lesson 14-3

NAME _____ COURSE _____ DATE _____

A. Transcribe what you hear on the accompanying audio disc into Chinese characters.

(1)

(2)

(3)

B. If a reference is given after a question, answer based on the referenced part of the Reading Exercises. If no reference is indicated, you may answer any way you wish.

(1) 那个美国人最后决定定一桌多少钱的酒席？
(那個美國人最後決定定一桌多少錢的酒席？) B1

(2) 张小姐明天打不打算参加那个酒席？席先生呢？
(張小姐明天打不打算參加那個酒席？席先生呢？) B2

(3) 你每天都做些什么？（你每天都做些甚麼？）

(4) 你以后要不要做买卖？（你以後要不要做買賣？）

. . . .

Reading and Writing Exercises for IWC Lesson 14-4

NAME _____   COURSE _____   DATE _____

A. **Transcribe what you hear on the accompanying audio disc into Chinese characters.**

(1)

(2)

(3)

B. **If a reference is given after a question, answer based on the referenced part of the Reading Exercises. If no reference is indicated, you may answer any way you wish.**

(1) 这个问题得由谁决定？（這個問題得由誰決定？）A4

(2) 何小山为什么自己一个人到加拿大留学去了？
（何小山為什麼自己一個人到加拿大留學去了？）A8

(3) 你比较喜欢吃什么风味的菜？（你比較喜歡吃甚麼風味的菜？）

(4) 你想不想到北京或者台北去留学？
（你想不想到北京或者台北去留學？）

. . . .

Reading and Writing Exercises for IWC Lesson 15-1

NAME _____ COURSE _____ DATE _____

A. Transcribe what you hear on the accompanying audio disc into Chinese characters.

(1)

(2)

(3)

B. If a reference is given after a question, answer based on the referenced part of the Reading Exercises. If no reference is indicated, you may answer any way you wish.

(1) 那家人喜欢过什么样的生活？
(那家人喜歡過什麼樣的生活？) C2

(2) 那个人觉得自己一个人生活怎么样？
(那個人覺得自己一個人生活怎麼樣？) C3

(3) 你平常几点钟吃晚饭？（你平常幾點鐘吃晚飯？）

(4) 你最喜欢说的一句中国话是什么？
(你最喜歡說的一句中國話是甚麼？)

Reading and Writing Exercises for IWC Lesson 15-2

NAME _____ COURSE _____ DATE _____

A. Transcribe what you hear on the accompanying audio disc into Chinese characters.

(1)

(2)

(3)

B. If a reference is given after a question, answer based on the referenced part of the Reading Exercises. If no reference is indicated, you may answer any way you wish.

(1) 各国的生活习惯都一样吗？（各國的生活習慣都一樣嗎？）A1

(2) 如果法国人家里有客人，他们会怎么样？
（如果法國人家裡有客人，他們會怎麼樣？）A8

(3) 你认识多少个中国字？（你認識多少個中國字？）

(4) 你每天学习几个钟头？（你每天學習幾個鐘頭？）

Reading and Writing Exercises for IWC Lesson 15-3

NAME _____ COURSE _____ DATE _____

A. Transcribe what you hear on the accompanying audio disc into Chinese characters.

(1)

(2)

(3)

B. If a reference is given after a question, answer based on the referenced part of the Reading Exercises. If no reference is indicated, you may answer any way you wish.

(1) 中国北方人习惯吃面，南方人更喜欢吃什么？你呢？
　　(中國北方人習慣吃麵，南方人更喜歡吃甚麼？你呢？) A2

(2) 他们现在生活过得那么好，应该感谢谁？
　　(他們現在生活過得那麼好，應該感謝誰？) A4

(3) 你是一个喜欢讲笑话的人吗？
　　(你是一個喜歡講笑話的人嗎？)

(4) 你常常把鞋子放在桌子上吗？
　　(你常常把鞋子放在桌子上嗎？)

Reading and Writing Exercises for IWC Lesson 15-4

NAME _____ COURSE _____ DATE _____

A. Transcribe what you hear on the accompanying audio disc into Chinese characters.

(1)

(2)

(3)

B. If a reference is given after a question, answer based on the referenced part of the Reading Exercises. If no reference is indicated, you may answer any way you wish.

(1) 除了小林和小方之外，还有别的同学愿意再去动物园吗？
  （除了小林和小方之外，還有別的同學願意再去動物園嗎？）A4

(2) 饺子馅儿里头都有什么？（餃子餡兒裡頭都有甚麼？）B1

(3) 你觉得张太太应当怎么办？（你覺得張太太應當怎麼辦？）C2

(4) 如果有人跟你说"让你久等了"，你会怎么跟他说？
  （如果有人跟你說"讓你久等了"，你會怎麼跟他說？）

Reading and Writing Exercises for IWC Lesson 16-1

NAME _____ COURSE _____ DATE _____

A. Transcribe what you hear on the accompanying audio disc into Chinese characters.

(1)

(2)

(3)

B. If a reference is given after a question, answer based on the referenced part of the Reading Exercises. If no reference is indicated, you may answer any way you wish.

(1) 说话的那个人要服务员做什么？
(說話的那個人要服務員做甚麼？) A5

(2) 那个人的表姐现在还在工厂里工作吗？
(那個人的表姐現在還在工廠裡工作嗎？) A6

(3) 和平饭店的服务好吗？ (和平飯店的服務好嗎？) B2

(4) 你是喜欢吃牛肉还是喜欢吃鱼？
(你是喜歡吃牛肉還是喜歡吃魚？)

Reading and Writing Exercises for IWC Lesson 16-2

NAME _____ COURSE _____ DATE _____

A. Transcribe what you hear on the accompanying audio disc into Chinese characters.

(1)

(2)

(3)

B. If a reference is given after a question, answer based on the referenced part of the Reading Exercises. If no reference is indicated, you may answer any way you wish.

(1) 学校前边的河很深，水里应该有很多鱼吧？
(學校前邊的河很深，水裡應該有很多魚吧？) A6

(2) 王大海跟他爸爸比起来，谁的酒量比较大？
(王大海跟他爸爸比起來，誰的酒量比較大？) A10

(3) 为什么那个人要替老简接风？
(為什麼那個人要替老簡接風？) C2

(4) 你要是去了中国，敢不敢开口跟中国人说中国话？
(你要是去了中國，敢不敢開口跟中國人說中國話？)

Reading and Writing Exercises for IWC Lesson 16-3

NAME _____   COURSE _____   DATE _____

A. Transcribe what you hear on the accompanying audio disc into Chinese characters.

(1)

(2)

(3)

B. If a reference is given after a question, answer based on the referenced part of the Reading Exercises. If no reference is indicated, you may answer any way you wish.

(1) 今天的天气预报怎么说？（今天的天氣預報怎麼說？）A6

(2) "饭后百步走，活到九十九"这句话是什么意思？
　　（"飯後百步走，活到九十九"這句話是什麼意思？）B3

(3) 小东的最爱是什么？（小東的最愛是甚麼？）C

(4) 你最近学习紧不紧张？（你最近學習緊不緊張？）

Reading and Writing Exercises for IWC Lesson 16-4

NAME _____ COURSE _____ DATE _____

A. Transcribe what you hear on the accompanying audio disc into Chinese characters.

(1)

(2)

(3)

B. If a reference is given after a question, answer based on the referenced part of the Reading Exercises. If no reference is indicated, you may answer any way you wish.

(1) 小李虽然没钱，可是很快乐，对不对？
（小李雖然沒錢，可是很快樂，對不對？） A2

(2) 有老师特别喜欢在饭馆儿上课，你觉得有没有关系？
（有老師特別喜歡在飯館兒上課，你覺得有沒有關係？）

(3) 如果有一个人以茶代酒，那么他最后喝的是茶还是酒？
（如果有一個人以茶代酒，那麼他最後喝的是茶還是酒？）

(4) 可口可乐和百事可乐，你喝得出来哪个是哪个吗？你比较喜欢
喝哪个？
（可口可樂和百事可樂，你喝得出來哪個是哪個嗎？你比較喜
歡喝哪個？）

Reading and Writing Exercises for IWC Lesson 17-1

NAME _____ COURSE _____ DATE _____

A. Transcribe what you hear on the accompanying audio disc into Chinese characters.

(1)

(2)

(3)

B. If a reference is given after a question, answer based on the referenced part of the Reading Exercises. If no reference is indicated, you may answer any way you wish.

(1) 最近几年，北京的空气怎么样？
(最近幾年，北京的空氣怎麼樣？) A2

(2) 今天晚上的音乐会，我们应该几点钟到比较好？
(今天晚上的音樂會，我們應該幾點鐘到比較好？) A6

(3) 你对国际关系感不感兴趣？（你對國際關係感不感興趣？）

(4) 今天晚上有音乐会，不知道你有没有空儿？
(今天晚上有音樂會，不知道你有沒有空兒？)

Reading and Writing Exercises for IWC Lesson 17-2

NAME_____ COURSE_____ DATE_____

A. Transcribe what you hear on the accompanying audio disc into Chinese characters.

(1)

(2)

(3)

B. If a reference is given after a question, answer based on the referenced part of the Reading Exercises. If no reference is indicated, you may answer any way you wish.

(1) 你觉得，文太太为什么挂电话了？
(你覺得，文太太為什麼挂電話了？) A2

(2) 说话的人要小毛做什么？(說話的人要小毛做甚麼？) A3

(3) 那个人要告诉他妹妹什么？(那個人要告訴他妹妹甚麼？) A6

(4) 要是你给朋友打电话但是电话占线，你怎么办？
(要是你給朋友打電話但是電話佔線，你怎麼辦？)

. . . .

Reading and Writing Exercises for IWC Lesson 17-3

NAME _____ COURSE _____ DATE _____

A. Transcribe what you hear on the accompanying audio disc into Chinese characters.

(1)

(2)

(3)

B. If a reference is given after a question, answer based on the referenced part of the Reading Exercises. If no reference is indicated, you may answer any way you wish.

(1) 那位美国领事的声调准不准？
(那位美國領事的聲調準不準？) A3

(2) 王大海叫我立刻去买什么？（王大海叫我立刻去買什麼？）A10

(3) 黄河为什么叫"黄河"？（黃河為什麼叫"黃河"？）C1

(4) 你平常是在图书馆学习还是在自己的房间学习？
(你平常是在圖書館學習還是在自己的房間學習？)

Reading and Writing Exercises for IWC Lesson 17-4

NAME _____ COURSE _____ DATE _____

A. Transcribe what you hear on the accompanying audio disc into Chinese characters.

(1)

(2)

(3)

B. If a reference is given after a question, answer based on the referenced part of the Reading Exercises. If no reference is indicated, you may answer any way you wish.

(1) 为什么有的香港的男人很坏？
(為什麼有的香港的男人很壞？) A7

(2) 谢太太看了金小姐的房子，特别喜欢什么？
(謝太太看了金小姐的房子，特別喜歡甚麼？) B4

(3) 你怕什么？（你怕甚麼？）

(4) 你房间里的床是单人床还是双人床？
(你房間裡的床是單人床還是雙人床？)

Reading and Writing Exercises for IWC Lesson 18-1

NAME _____ COURSE _____ DATE _____

A. Transcribe what you hear on the accompanying audio disc into Chinese characters.

(1)

(2)

(3)

B. If a reference is given after a question, answer based on the referenced part of the Reading Exercises. If no reference is indicated, you may answer any way you wish.

(1) 为什么需要马上解决这个问题？
(為什麼需要馬上解決這個問題？) A6

(2) 最近几年中美关系怎么样？(最近幾年中美關係怎麼樣？) A8

(3) 作者觉得做爸爸、妈妈的应该管什么？
(作者覺得做爸爸、媽媽的應該管甚麼？) C1

(4) 你以后要不要孩子？如果你想要的话，你要几个？
(你以後要不要孩子？如果你想要的話，你要幾個？)

Reading and Writing Exercises for IWC Lesson 18-2

NAME _____ COURSE _____ DATE _____

A. Transcribe what you hear on the accompanying audio disc into Chinese characters.

(1)

(2)

(3)

B. If a reference is given after a question, answer based on the referenced part of the Reading Exercises. If no reference is indicated, you may answer any way you wish.

(1) 张先生打算改天做什么？（張先生打算改天做甚麼？）A7

(2) 既然饭馆的菜不怎么样，他们就决定做什么了？
(既然飯館的菜不怎麼樣，他們就決定做甚麼了？) A8

(3) 一位大使在哪儿工作？一位领事呢？
(一位大使在哪兒工作？一位領事呢？)

(4) 你的生日那天，你希望朋友们送给你什么东西？
(你的生日那天，你希望朋友們送給你什麼東西？)

Reading and Writing Exercises for IWC Lesson 18-3

NAME _____   COURSE _____   DATE _____

A. Transcribe what you hear on the accompanying audio disc into Chinese characters.

(1)

(2)

(3)

B. If a reference is given after a question, answer based on the referenced part of the Reading Exercises. If no reference is indicated, you may answer any way you wish.

(1) 有的时候中国人对不可能的事情会怎么样？
(有的時候中國人對不可能的事情會怎麼樣？) c1

(2) 作者特别不喜欢的事情是什么？
(作者特別不喜歡的事情是甚麼？) c3

(3) 你抽不抽烟？（你抽不抽煙？）

(4) 如果有一个好朋友来找你，对你说："有点小事情，想请你帮
个忙"，你会怎么说？
(如果有一個好朋友來找你，對你說："有點小事情，想請你
幫個忙"，你會怎麼說？)

Reading and Writing Exercises for IWC Lesson 18-4

NAME _____   COURSE _____   DATE _____

A. Transcribe what you hear on the accompanying audio disc into Chinese characters.

(1)

(2)

(3)

B. If a reference is given after a question, answer based on the referenced part of the Reading Exercises. If no reference is indicated, you may answer any way you wish.

(1) 说话的那个人保证什么？（說話的那個人保證什麼？）A2

(2) 那位中国女同学对什么特别感兴趣？
（那位中國女同學對甚麼特別感興趣？）C2

(3) 她想找一位日本女同学做什么？
（她想找一位日本女同學做甚麼？）C2

(4) 中文学起来很容易吧？（中文學起來很容易吧？）

Reading and Writing Exercises for IWC Lesson 19-1

NAME _____   COURSE _____   DATE _____

A. Transcribe what you hear on the accompanying audio disc into Chinese characters.

(1)

(2)

(3)

B. If a reference is given after a question, answer based on the referenced part of the Reading Exercises. If no reference is indicated, you may answer any way you wish.

(1) 王明力为什么决定这次要坐船？
    （王明力為什麼決定這次要坐船？）B2

(2) 你常生病吗？（你常生病嗎？）

(3) 你怕不怕考试？（你怕不怕考試？）

(4) 你每天都跑步吗？（你每天都跑步嗎？）

. . . .

Reading and Writing Exercises for IWC Lesson 19-2

NAME _____ COURSE _____ DATE _____

A. Transcribe what you hear on the accompanying audio disc into Chinese characters.

(1)

(2)

(3)

B. If a reference is given after a question, answer based on the referenced part of the Reading Exercises. If no reference is indicated, you may answer any way you wish.

(1) 学中文的学生一定得注意什么？
(學中文的學生一定得注意甚麼？) A3

(2) 小严的论文是关于什么的？（小嚴的論文是關於甚麼的？）B5

(3) 你身体好吗？（你身體好嗎？）

(4) 你上高中的时候，成绩不错吧？
(你上高中的時候，成績不錯吧？)

Reading and Writing Exercises for IWC Lesson 19-3

NAME _____ COURSE _____ DATE _____

A. Transcribe what you hear on the accompanying audio disc into Chinese characters.

(1)

(2)

(3)

B. If a reference is given after a question, answer based on the referenced part of the Reading Exercises. If no reference is indicated, you may answer any way you wish.

(1) 请你提三种主义。(請你提三種主義。) A7

(2) 这位女生的男朋友告诉她他交了别的女朋友，讲完话以后，有没有看她一眼？
(這位女生的男朋友告訴她他交了別的女朋友，講完話以後，有沒有看她一眼？) C1

(3) 你的中文讲得很流利吧？(你的中文講得很流利吧？)

(4) 你是比较内向的人还是比较外向的人？
(你是比較內向的人還是比較外向的人？)

Reading and Writing Exercises for IWC Lesson 19-4

NAME _____ COURSE _____ DATE _____

A. Transcribe what you hear on the accompanying audio disc into Chinese characters.

(1)

(2)

(3)

B. If a reference is given after a question, answer based on the referenced part of the Reading Exercises. If no reference is indicated, you may answer any way you wish.

(1) 任万里的父母在哪儿教书？（任萬里的父母在哪兒教書？）c1

(2) 作者的父母尽了父母应尽的责任吗？
（作者的父母盡了父母應盡的責任嗎？）c2

(3) 你常给父母写信吗？（你常給父母寫信嗎？）

(4) 父母当然对孩子有责任，你相信孩子对父母也有责任吗？
（父母當然對孩子有責任，你相信孩子對父母也有責任嗎？）

Reading and Writing Exercises for IWC Lesson 20-1

NAME _____ COURSE _____ DATE _____

A. Transcribe what you hear on the accompanying audio disc into Chinese characters.

(1)

(2)

(3)

B. If a reference is given after a question, answer based on the referenced part of the Reading Exercises. If no reference is indicated, you may answer any way you wish.

(1) 那个人的爱好是什么？（那個人的愛好是甚麼？）A1

(2) 他们要参观什么样的工厂？（他們要參觀甚麼樣的工廠？）A5

(3) 严小姐为什么用 "怪不得" 三个字？
（嚴小姐為什麼用 "怪不得" 三個字？）B3

(4) 你唱歌儿唱得怎么样？（你唱歌兒唱得怎麼樣？）

· ·

Reading and Writing Exercises for IWC Lesson 20-2

NAME _____   COURSE _____   DATE _____

A. Transcribe what you hear on the accompanying audio disc into Chinese characters.

(1)

(2)

(3)

B. If a reference is given after a question, answer based on the referenced part of the Reading Exercises. If no reference is indicated, you may answer any way you wish.

(1) 中华人民共和国的第一大报叫什么？
（中華人民共和國的第一大報叫什麼？）A1

(2) 华国树的母亲对什么很有研究？
（華國樹的母親對甚麼很有研究？）A2

(3) 你的父母亲住在哪里？（你的父母親住在哪裏？）

(4) 中文报纸你看得懂吗？（中文報紙你看得懂嗎？）

Reading and Writing Exercises for IWC Lesson 20-3

NAME _____ COURSE _____ DATE _____

A. Transcribe what you hear on the accompanying audio disc into Chinese characters.

(1)

(2)

(3)

B. If a reference is given after a question, answer based on the referenced part of the Reading Exercises. If no reference is indicated, you may answer any way you wish.

(1) 《月的主人》是比较新的电影，对不对？
(《月的主人》是比較新的電影，對不對？) B1

(2) 哥哥和弟弟有什么不一样的地方吗？
(哥哥和弟弟有甚麼不一樣的地方嗎？) C1

(3) 你将来有什么计划？（你將來有甚麼計劃？）

(4) 你比较喜欢自己说故事，还是比较喜欢听别人说故事？
(你比較喜歡自己說故事，還是比較喜歡聽別人說故事？)

. . . .

Reading and Writing Exercises for IWC Lesson 20-4

NAME _____ COURSE _____ DATE _____

A. Transcribe what you hear on the accompanying audio disc into Chinese characters.

(1)

(2)

(3)

B. If a reference is given after a question, answer based on the referenced part of the Reading Exercises. If no reference is indicated, you may answer any way you wish.

(1) 那个人忘了什么？（那個人忘了甚麼？）A1

(2) 美国老一代的华人，大部分是从中国什么地方来的？
（美國老一代的華人，大部分是從中國甚麼地方來的？）A4

(3) 那三个人决定学什么专业？（那三個人決定學甚麼專業？）

(4) 你住的房间在几楼？（你住的房間在幾樓？）

Reading and Writing Exercises for IWC Lesson 21-1

NAME _____   COURSE _____   DATE _____

A. Transcribe what you hear on the accompanying audio disc into Chinese characters.

(1)

(2)

(3)

B. If a reference is given after a question, answer based on the referenced part of the Reading Exercises. If no reference is indicated, you may answer any way you wish.

(1) 王大海用不用功？他妹妹呢？ A10

(2) 那个老外以前打什么球？打得好不好？你是怎么知道的？
(那個老外以前打甚麼球？打得好不好？你是怎麼知道的？) B1

(3) 你喜欢做哪些运动？(你喜歡做哪些運動？)

(4) 你这个学期有没有室友？(你這個學期有沒有室友？)

Reading and Writing Exercises for IWC Lesson 21-2

NAME _____ COURSE _____ DATE _____

A. Transcribe what you hear on the accompanying audio disc into Chinese characters.

(1)

(2)

(3)

B. If a reference is given after a question, answer based on the referenced part of the Reading Exercises. If no reference is indicated, you may answer any way you wish.

(1) 那个人的室友加入了几个社团？你加入了几个？
(那個人的室友加入了幾個社團？你加入了幾個？) A9

(2) 王大海的专业是教育吗？(王大海的專業是教育嗎？) A10

(3) 那个台湾同学几点钟在哪里等他的美国同学？
(那個台灣同學幾點鐘在哪裡等他的美國同學？) B1

(4) 假如你有一百万元的话，你会怎么花？
(假如你有一百萬元的話，你會怎麼花？)

Reading and Writing Exercises for IWC Lesson 21-3

NAME _____ COURSE _____ DATE _____

A. Transcribe what you hear on the accompanying audio disc into Chinese characters.

(1)

(2)

(3)

B. If a reference is given after a question, answer based on the referenced part of the Reading Exercises. If no reference is indicated, you may answer any way you wish.

(1) 哪个足球队比较强？（哪個足球隊比較強？）A3

(2) 黄河是世界上最长的河吗？（黃河是世界上最長的河嗎？）A7

(3) 你喜欢看足球吗？（你喜歡看足球嗎？）

(4) 你最喜欢看的电视节目是哪个？
（你最喜歡看的電視節目是哪個？）

Reading and Writing Exercises for IWC Lesson 21-4

NAME _____ COURSE _____ DATE _____

A. Transcribe what you hear on the accompanying audio disc into Chinese characters.

(1)

(2)

(3)

B. If a reference is given after a question, answer based on the referenced part of the Reading Exercises. If no reference is indicated, you may answer any way you wish.

(1) 万里长城是什么时候修建的？
(萬里長城是什麼時候修建的？) A1

(2) 你觉得爱情可靠不可靠？房子是不是比男人更可靠？
(你覺得愛情可靠不可靠？房子是不是比男人更可靠？) A7

(3) 那部电影是哪一类的电影？是关于什么的？
(那部電影是哪一類的電影？是關於甚麼的？) A8

(4) 长城到底有多长？（長城到底有多長？）

Reading and Writing Exercises for IWC Lesson 22-1

NAME _____   COURSE _____   DATE _____

A. Transcribe what you hear on the accompanying audio disc into Chinese characters.

(1)

(2)

(3)

B. If a reference is given after a question, answer based on the referenced part of the Reading Exercises. If no reference is indicated, you may answer any way you wish.

(1) 高英华夫人是不是说过广州过几年一定还有更大的变化？
（高英華夫人是不是說過廣州過幾年一定還有更大的變化？）B2

(2) 许志明同志觉得英国的医生怎么样？英国的医院怎么样？
（許志明同志覺得英國的醫生怎麼樣？英國的醫院怎麼樣？）C1

(3) 你相信气候变化吗？（你相信氣候變化嗎？）

(4) 离你家最近的电影院叫什么？
（離你家最近的電影院叫甚麼？）

. . . .

Reading and Writing Exercises for IWC Lesson 22-2

NAME _____   COURSE _____   DATE _____

A. Transcribe what you hear on the accompanying audio disc into Chinese characters.

(1)

(2)

(3)

B. If a reference is given after a question, answer based on the referenced part of the Reading Exercises. If no reference is indicated, you may answer any way you wish.

(1) 他们为什么得快一点儿赶到车站？
　　（他們為什麼得快一點兒趕到車站？）A8

(2) 王大海有什么问题？（王大海有甚麼問題？）A10

(3) 你有几双皮鞋？（你有幾雙皮鞋？）

(4) 你每天读几个小时书？（你每天讀幾個小時書？）

Reading and Writing Exercises for IWC Lesson 22-3

NAME _____ COURSE _____ DATE _____

 A. Transcribe what you hear on the accompanying audio disc into Chinese characters.

(1)

(2)

(3)

B. If a reference is given after a question, answer based on the referenced part of the Reading Exercises. If no reference is indicated, you may answer any way you wish.

(1) 那个地方为什么很危险？（那個地方為什麼很危險？）A6

(2) 他们把皮包还给马南喜以前，要她先做什么？
（他們把皮包還給馬南喜以前，要她先做甚麼？）B1

(3) 你觉得，完全忘掉自己的"根"有没有关系？
（你覺得，完全忘掉自己的"根"有沒有關係？）C2

(4) 你喜欢坐火车还是坐飞机？（你喜歡坐火車還是坐飛機？）

Reading and Writing Exercises for IWC Lesson 22-4

NAME _____   COURSE _____   DATE _____

A. Transcribe what you hear on the accompanying audio disc into Chinese characters.

(1)

(2)

(3)

B. If a reference is given after a question, answer based on the referenced part of the Reading Exercises. If no reference is indicated, you may answer any way you wish.

(1) 她考试的结果怎么样？（她考試的結果怎麼樣？）A4

(2) 为什么住校外不太合算？（為什麼住校外不太合算？）A9

(3) 那个中国人受伤了吗？他的衣服怎么样？
（那個中國人受傷了嗎？他的衣服怎麼樣？）B1

(4) 你说中国话，是不是很注意发音？
（你說中國話，是不是很注意發音？）

Reading and Writing Exercises for IWC Lesson 23-1

NAME _____   COURSE _____   DATE _____

A. Transcribe what you hear on the accompanying audio disc into Chinese characters.

(1)

(2)

(3)

B. If a reference is given after a question, answer based on the referenced part of the Reading Exercises. If no reference is indicated, you may answer any way you wish.

(1) 加拿大是由几个省组成的？（加拿大是由幾個省組成的？）A1

(2) 这个女孩儿出生时，左手原来有几个手指头？现在呢？
（這個女孩兒出生時，左手原來有幾個手指頭？現在呢？）A7

(3) 香港人五十年之內可以过高度民主、自由的生活，并且怎么样？
（香港人五十年之內可以過高度民主、自由的生活，並且怎麼樣？）A8

(4) 你觉得哪种经济制度比较好，市场经济还是计划经济？
（你覺得哪種經濟制度比較好，市場經濟還是計劃經濟？）

Reading and Writing Exercises for IWC Lesson 23-2

NAME _____ COURSE _____ DATE _____

A. Transcribe what you hear on the accompanying audio disc into Chinese characters.

(1)

(2)

(3)

B. If a reference is given after a question, answer based on the referenced part of the Reading Exercises. If no reference is indicated, you may answer any way you wish.

(1) 哪一家银行在世界各国银行里排名第一？
（哪一家銀行在世界各國銀行裏排名第一？）A6

(2) 比较大的商店完全不可能讲价吗？
（比較大的商店完全不可能講價嗎？）B1

(3) 你觉得应不应该保存传统文化？
（你覺得應不應該保存傳統文化？）

(4) 如果光吃肉，一点儿菜或水果都不吃，对身体不太好吧？
（如果光吃肉，一點兒菜或水果都不吃，對身體不太好吧？）

· ·

Reading and Writing Exercises for IWC Lesson 23-3

NAME _____   COURSE _____   DATE _____

A. Transcribe what you hear on the accompanying audio disc into Chinese characters.

(1)

(2)

(3)

B. If a reference is given after a question, answer based on the referenced part of the Reading Exercises. If no reference is indicated, you may answer any way you wish.

(1) 中国很多年以来实行什么样的人口政策？
　　(中國很多年以來實行甚麼樣的人口政策？) A7

(2) 香港的小学和中学，基本上都用什么语言来上课？
　　(香港的小學和中學，基本上都用甚麼語言來上課？) B

(3) 你周六、周日平常都做些什么呢？
　　(你週六、週日平常都做些甚麼呢？)

(4) 普通话是中国的官方语言。在你看来，美国需不需要一种官方语言？
　　(普通話是中國的官方語言。在你看來，美國需不需要一種官方語言？)

Reading and Writing Exercises for IWC Lesson 23-4

NAME _____ COURSE _____ DATE _____

A. Transcribe what you hear on the accompanying audio disc into Chinese characters.

(1)

(2)

(3)

B. If a reference is given after a question, answer based on the referenced part of the Reading Exercises. If no reference is indicated, you may answer any way you wish.

(1) 林业为什么在中国的东北特别发达？
   (林業為什麼在中國的東北特別發達？) A5

(2) 谁是美国历史上最年轻的总统？
   (誰是美國歷史上最年輕的總統？) C1

(3) 小偷进了那个外国人的家，他听到的第一句话是什么？
   (小偷進了那個外國人的家，他聽到的第一句話是甚麼？) C4

(4) 你有没有兴趣将来给美国政府做事？
   (你有沒有興趣將來給美國政府做事？)

....

Reading and Writing Exercises for IWC Lesson 24-1

NAME _____   COURSE _____   DATE _____

A. Transcribe what you hear on the accompanying audio disc into Chinese characters.

(1)

(2)

(3)

B. If a reference is given after a question, answer based on the referenced part of the Reading Exercises. If no reference is indicated, you may answer any way you wish.

(1) 根据2010年的美国人口调查，美国有多少人是华人？
(根據2010年的美國人口調查，美國有多少人是華人？) A3

(2) 新加坡的华语为什么带有一点本地方言的音调？
(新加坡的華語為什麼帶有一點本地方言的音調？) A9

(3) 在新加坡，大部分的人可以使用几种语言？
(在新加坡，大部分的人可以使用幾種語言？) B

(4) 你决定学习中文，有没有受到谁的影响？
(你決定學習中文，有沒有受到誰的影響？)

· ·

Reading and Writing Exercises for IWC Lesson 24-2

NAME _____   COURSE _____   DATE _____

A. Transcribe what you hear on the accompanying audio disc into Chinese characters.

(1)

(2)

(3)

B. If a reference is given after a question, answer based on the referenced part of the Reading Exercises. If no reference is indicated, you may answer any way you wish.

(1) 老虎为什么已经到了快要绝种的地步了？
　　(老虎為什麼已經到了快要絕種的地步了？) A8

(2) 回民有时候也吃猪肉吗？
　　(回民有時候也吃豬肉嗎？) C1

(3) 你每天都喝牛奶吗？ (你每天都喝牛奶嗎？)

(4) 你觉得保护自然环境很重要吗？
　　(你覺得保護自然環境很重要嗎？)

Reading and Writing Exercises for IWC Lesson 24-3

NAME _____ COURSE _____ DATE _____

A. Transcribe what you hear on the accompanying audio disc into Chinese characters.

(1)

(2)

(3)

B. If a reference is given after a question, answer based on the referenced part of the Reading Exercises. If no reference is indicated, you may answer any way you wish.

(1) 再过十年，世界上人口最多的国家可能是哪一国？
(再過十年，世界上人口最多的國家可能是哪一國？) A3

(2) 新加坡是哪年独立的？(新加坡是哪年獨立的？) A6

(3) 你缺少什么东西？(你缺少甚麼東西？)

(4) 在美国，科学家的收入高，还是律师的收入高？
(在美國，科學家的收入高，還是律師的收入高？)

Reading and Writing Exercises for IWC Lesson 24-4

NAME _____ COURSE _____ DATE _____

A. Transcribe what you hear on the accompanying audio disc into Chinese characters.

(1)

(2)

(3)

B. If a reference is given after a question, answer based on the referenced part of the Reading Exercises. If no reference is indicated, you may answer any way you wish.

(1) 根据毛主席说的话，世界历史是谁创造的？
（根據毛主席說的話，世界歷史是誰創造的？）A4

(2) 那个人想买什么？（那個人想買甚麼？）A6

(3) 早在两千多年前，中国人就发明了什么东西？
（早在兩千多年前，中國人就發明了甚麼東西？）C1

(4) 你什么时候穿运动装？（你什麼時候穿運動裝？）

Translation Exercises for *Intermediate Written Chinese* Units 11-24

. . . .

Translation Exercises for IWC Unit 11

NAME _____ COURSE _____ DATE _____

Instructions: Translate the following into Chinese characters. If you have forgotten a word or character, check in the corresponding lesson of your textbook or consult the glossaries.

(1) Driver, please drive a little slower!

(2) Little Wang, walk a little faster!

(3) Relax, this problem has already been solved.

(4) That foreigner hasn't taken a bus for a long time.

(5) I'm already finished eating. I suppose you've also finished eating?

(6) I looked all over. No matter how hard I looked, I couldn't find that furniture store.

(7) I tell you, the house I live in is on the left side, not on the right side.

(8) Quickly look for a gas station. We have to refuel again.

(9) I guess it would be better after all to fill it up.

(10) Starting last year, the price of gasoline has been getting more and more expensive.

Translation Exercises for IWC Unit 12

NAME _____ COURSE _____ DATE _____

Instructions: Translate the following into Chinese characters. If you have forgotten a word or character, check in the corresponding lesson of your textbook or consult the glossaries.

(1) Is he majoring in astronomy or biology?

(2) She wants to study French or Japanese.

(3) That Canadian doesn't know what to do *at all*!

(4) I'd like to buy a Chinese newspaper and 100 sheets of paper.

(5) These notebooks are mine. Those notebooks are whose?

(6)   This book, where did you buy it? In China they don't sell this kind of book!

(7)   How come cabbage has recently been so expensive?

(8)   These vegetables only arrived this morning. (I) guarantee they taste good.

(9)   The fruit, please wrap it up, thank you.

(10) Peking University is much richer than Beijing Language & Culture University.

Translation Exercises for IWC Unit 13

NAME _____   COURSE _____   DATE _____

Instructions: Translate the following into Chinese characters. If you have forgotten a word or character, check in the corresponding lesson of your textbook or consult the glossaries.

(1)   That grocery store is extremely close, not far away at all.

(2)   Please cut a kilo of beef for me.

(3)   I want to buy cabbage, fruit, white bread, and so forth.

(4)   To save money, he decided not to eat lunch.

(5)   Here is the exit, not the entrance!

(6)   This pair of shoes is different from that pair of shoes.

(7)   She likes to wear white shoes. She doesn't like to wear black shoes.

(8)   It's pretty, all right, but it's too expensive. Could you reduce the price a little?

(9)   If the sweater is too small, within 30 days you can bring it here for exchange.

(10) Size 11 should be fine. (lit. "Wearing size 11 there should be no problem.")

Translation Exercises for IWC Unit 14

NAME _____   COURSE _____   DATE _____

Instructions: Translate the following into Chinese characters. If you have forgotten a word or character, check in the corresponding lesson of your textbook or consult the glossaries.

(1)   As you wish. It doesn't matter which (kind of) language you use.

(2)   Her dad and mom said that A- is not good enough.

(3)   Don't drink so much alcohol! (lit. "Drink a little less liquor!")

(4)   It's OK even if you put on more. (lit. "Putting on a little more also doesn't matter.")

(5)   We also want 6 ounces of rice. We have an urgent matter. Please bring the food faster.

(6)   This Chinese friend of mine can't stand the weather here.

(7)   I'd like to reserve 8 tables for a banquet; one where each person costs 90 yuan.

(8)   There will be about 100 people participating. Please make preparations early.

(9)   I myself like to eat Hunanese-flavored cuisine.

(10) This matter, let it be decided by those study-abroad students themselves.

Translation Exercises for IWC Unit 15

NAME _____   COURSE _____   DATE _____

Instructions: Translate the following into Chinese characters. If you have forgotten a word or character, check in the corresponding lesson of your textbook or consult the glossaries.

(1) I'll first simply say a few words.

(2) I'm extremely happy to have the chance to come here and live together with everyone.

(3) This place, the longer I live (here), the more I get accustomed (to it).

(4) I and the school president became acquainted long ago.

(5) Today you're all guests. Please each of you eat more and drink more!

(6)   Thank you very much, Mr. Zhang, Mrs. Zhang!

(7)   First put vegetables on it. Then take the meat and put it in the middle.

(8)   He can tell jokes better than I can.

(9)   Besides meat, inside there is also cabbage and condiments.

(10) Of course I'd be willing to go. Will you let me go?

Translation Exercises for IWC Unit 16

NAME _____   COURSE _____   DATE _____

Instructions: Translate the following into Chinese characters. If you have forgotten a word or character, check in the corresponding lesson of your textbook or consult the glossaries.

(1)   Waiter, we'd like to order. Do you have fish today?

(2)   It's embarrassing to let you treat me. Next time I'll be the host!

(3)   Today, it's not only very cold, but also very dry.

(4)   We'll have a welcome dinner Friday night for Old Shi.

(5)   The water in the lake is very deep, and there are many rocks in the water.

(6)   What (how) does the weather forecast say?

(7)   Your little sister is very cute! How old is she?

(8)   Don't be nervous. My math isn't very good either.

(9) I can't drink liquor. I'll drink tea as a substitute for liquor.

(10) Though the food here isn't as good as in a restaurant, you still should eat some more!

Translation Exercises for IWC Unit 17

NAME _____   COURSE _____   DATE _____

Instructions: Translate the following into Chinese characters. If you have forgotten a word or character, check in the corresponding lesson of your textbook or consult the glossaries.

(1)   I'm interested in music. Are you interested in music too?

(2)   Don't mention it. We all know the air today is bad.

(3)   The school has 97 Chinese students and 69 international students.

(4)   The minute I call he hangs up! I have no choice but to use a FAX machine.

(5)   I tell you, her phone is always busy. What should I do?

(6)   Ms. Huang, please go to the consulate immediately!

(7)   In the library you may not speak in a loud voice.

(8)   He likes to drink red wine. She likes to drink white wine.

(9)   They should plant some trees, flowers, and grass, then it will be prettier.

(10) That room has some simple furniture like a bed, a desk, and so on.

Translation Exercises for IWC Unit 18

NAME_____ COURSE_____ DATE_____

Instructions: Translate the following into Chinese characters. If you have forgotten a word or character, check in the corresponding lesson of your textbook or consult the glossaries.

(1) The kind of problems you're talking about are already rather serious.

(2) Children, one definitely has to control (them). I will immediately go control (them).

(3) Since you're so busy, let's chat while we eat.

(4) The ambassador hopes there will be international peace.

(5) Goodbye, see you tomorrow. I won't see you out. Take care!

(6) Please don't smoke. This is a non-smoking section.

(7) There is a matter (in which I) would like to ask you to help.

(8) Cultural exchange is very important, right?

(9) I'll definitely do my best to help you. Please relax.

(10) This matter is not easy to deal with, but I'll do my best, by golly.

Translation Exercises for IWC Unit 19

NAME _____   COURSE _____   DATE _____

Instructions: Translate the following into Chinese characters. If you have forgotten a word or character, check in the corresponding lesson of your textbook or consult the glossaries.

(1) He finished taking the exam and then he got sick.

(2) Children always like to run all over the place.

(3) I prefer taking ships. I don't like very much to take planes.

(4) My thesis is about comparative literature. What is your thesis about?

(5) (You) should pay attention to (your) health (body)!

(6) China and Vietnam are both communist countries.

(7) It's possible that the spoken language of extroverted students is relatively more fluent.

(8) Time passes really quickly. Blink your eyes and then a year (has passed).

(9) Although the job's responsibilities are heavy, I believe I can fulfill the responsibilities.

(10) Her parents both teach at Shanghai No. 23 Middle School.

Translation Exercises for IWC Unit 20

NAME _____   COURSE _____   DATE _____

Instructions: Translate the following into Chinese characters. If you have forgotten a word or character, check in the corresponding lesson of your textbook or consult the glossaries.

(1) I like to sing and paint. What are your hobbies?

(2) You say they went to visit a factory? No wonder I haven't seen them today!

(3) Sir, please help me take a photo. All right?

(4) There are many things that even graduate students don't understand.

(5) My father told her Shanghai is the capital of the People's Republic of China!

(6) Excuse me, in the future what plans do you have?

(7) That new movie tells the story of an American musician in the 1960s.

(8) I've never ever seen this type of film before.

(9) The seats are not bad: upstairs, row 1, numbers 7 and 8.

(10) That romantic film I've seen three times, but the main content I still don't understand.

Translation Exercises for IWC Unit 21

NAME_____ COURSE_____ DATE_____

Instructions: Translate the following into Chinese characters. If you have forgotten a word or character, check in the corresponding lesson of your textbook or consult the glossaries.

(1) Her luck is often bad. Her roommate's luck, on the other hand, is extremely good.

(2) He participates in three ball teams, but his schoolwork is good, so it's OK.

(3) See you tomorrow morning at 8:00 sharp in front of the gymnasium!

(4) Last spring her roommate joined thirteen clubs—really too many!

(5) If there's vacation on that day, I want to stay at home and do homework.

(6) Those three soccer teams are all world-famous, strong teams.

(7) I'll watch whichever television program you watch.

(8) You know, that war film is quite intense.

(9) At home you depend on (your) parents. When you go out, you depend on friends.

(10) Now, after all, during what period *was* the Great Wall really constructed?

Translation Exercises for IWC Unit 22

NAME _____   COURSE _____   DATE _____

Instructions: Translate the following into Chinese characters. If you have forgotten a word or character, check in the corresponding lesson of your textbook or consult the glossaries.

(1)   Male comrades sit here. Female comrades sit there!

(2)   That hospital has several doctors who understand English.

(3)   Maybe the problem of climate change can still be solved.

(4)   Her purse, passport, and various kinds of identification papers were all stolen.

(5)   Tomorrow there's a test. You quickly go to the library to study!

(6)   Last Friday when I took the train, I lost my purse.

(7)   If (they) inspect it first, then there shouldn't be any danger.

(8)   Last week she got hurt and her clothes were torn.

(9)   Little Fei didn't take care of his own wallet, and as a result it got stolen.

(10) Give him some repair money. To wait for someone to come is not very worthwhile.

. . . .

Translation Exercises for IWC Unit 23

NAME _____　COURSE _____　DATE _____

Instructions: Translate the following into Chinese characters. If you have forgotten a word or character, check in the corresponding lesson of your textbook or consult the glossaries.

(1)　Hong Kong can be democratic and free. Moreover, its economic system won't change.

(2)　Could I ask, the People's Republic of China is composed of how many provinces?

(3)　My name is Li. Pleased to meet you. I'm willing to voluntarily serve as your guide.

(4)　Hong Kong takes banking, industry, and commerce as the most important things.

(5)　We must preserve traditional Chinese culture!

(6) China's official language is none other than Putonghua.

(7) Hong Kong has implemented mother tongue educational policy. Schools basically use the students' native language in class.

(8) I'm interested in Chinese geography, history, language, and culture—all of them.

(9) How many countries are there in the world that could be considered developed countries?

(10) The American government welcomes the Chinese government to send someone to participate in this informal meeting.

Translation Exercises for IWC Unit 24

NAME _____   COURSE _____   DATE _____

Instructions: Translate the following into Chinese characters. If you have forgotten a word or character, check in the corresponding lesson of your textbook or consult the glossaries.

(1)   The total population of Vietnam is 90 million, of which approximately 2% are Chinese.

(2)   The Chinese language in Taiwan has been influenced by the dialects there (lit. in this place).

(3)   So far as I know, the Beijing Zoo was founded in 1906.

(4)   That little tiger has absolutely not been weaned yet.

(5)   Due to the natural environment's having been continuously destroyed, China's tigers have already reached the point where they will soon die out.

(6)   Why do you say that India lacks scientists and lawyers?

(7)   That is an independent middle school. It accepts only female students.

(8)   Where was this desktop computer manufactured?

(9)   Tomorrow I'm going to a clothing store to buy some new athletic wear.

(10) I'd like to buy one of those newest model computers that can connect to the Internet via Wi-Fi.

Cornelius C. Kubler is Stanfield Professor of Asian Studies at Williams College, where he teaches Chinese and for many years chaired the Department of Asian Studies. On leave from Williams, he is currently serving as American Co-Director of the Johns Hopkins-Nanjing University Center for Chinese and American Studies in Nanjing, China. He was formerly Chinese Language Training Supervisor and Chair of the Department of Asian and African Languages at the Foreign Service Institute, U.S. Department of State, where he trained American diplomats in Chinese and other languages, and he served for six years as Principal of the American Institute in Taiwan Chinese Language & Area Studies School. Kubler, who has directed intensive Chinese language training programs in the U.S., mainland China, and Taiwan, has been active in Chinese language test development and has authored or coauthored 20 books and over 50 articles on Chinese language pedagogy and linguistics.

Jerling Guo Kubler, who was born and raised in Taiwan as the daughter of Beijing émigré parents, is a graduate of the Department of Foreign Languages and Literatures of Soochow University in Taipei. Her experience in language education spans four decades. She has taught all levels of Chinese as a Second/Foreign Language from pre-kindergarten to university level at institutions in Taiwan and the U.S. including Taipei Language Institute, Eisenhower College, and Williams College.

The Tuttle Story: "Books to Span the East and West"

Many people are surprised to learn that the world's leading publisher of books on Asia had humble beginnings in the tiny American state of Vermont. The company's founder, Charles E. Tuttle, belonged to a New England family steeped in publishing.

Tuttle's father was a noted antiquarian book dealer in Rutland, Vermont. Young Charles honed his knowledge of the trade working in the family bookstore, and later in the rare books section of Columbia University Library. His passion for beautiful books—old and new—never wavered throughout his long career as a bookseller and publisher.

After graduating from Harvard, Tuttle enlisted in the military and in 1945 was sent to Tokyo to work on General Douglas MacArthur's staff. He was tasked with helping to revive the Japanese publishing industry, which had been utterly devastated by the war. When his tour of duty was completed, he left the military, married a talented and beautiful singer, Reiko Chiba, and in 1948 began several successful business ventures.

To his astonishment, Tuttle discovered that postwar Tokyo was actually a book-lover's paradise. He befriended dealers in the Kanda district and began supplying rare Japanese editions to American libraries. He also imported American books to sell to the thousands of GIs stationed in Japan. By 1949, Tuttle's business was thriving, and he opened Tokyo's very first English-language bookstore in the Takashimaya Department Store in Nihonbashi, to great success. Two years later, he began publishing books to fulfill the growing interest of foreigners in all things Asian.

Though a westerner, Tuttle was hugely instrumental in bringing a knowledge of Japan and Asia to a world hungry for information about the East. By the time of his death in 1993, he had published over 6,000 books on Asian culture, history and art—a legacy honored by Emperor Hirohito in 1983 with the "Order of the Sacred Treasure," the highest honor Japan can bestow upon a non-Japanese.

The Tuttle company today maintains an active backlist of some 1,500 titles, many of which have been continuously in print since the 1950s and 1960s—a great testament to Charles Tuttle's skill as a publisher. More than 60 years after its founding, Tuttle Publishing is more active today than at any time in its history, still inspired by Charles Tuttle's core mission—to publish fine books to span the East and West and provide a greater understanding of each.